Step-by-Step French

From Alphabet to Conversation

Chloe S.

My First Picture Book Inc.

Copyright © 2024 by My First Picture Book Inc.

All rights reserved.

No portion of this book may be reproduced in any form without written permission from the publisher or author, except as permitted by U.S. copyright law.

Contents

1. Introduction to French — 1
2. The French Alphabet — 4
3. Pronunciation Guide — 8
4. Basic Greetings and Introductions — 12
5. Numbers and Counting — 17
6. Days of the Week — 22
7. Months and Seasons — 27
8. Colors — 33
9. Family Members — 38
10. Common Professions — 44
11. Basic Grammar Rules — 49
12. Articles and Gender — 54
13. Singular and Plural Nouns — 59
14. Subject Pronouns — 64
15. Possessive Adjectives — 69
16. Question Words — 75
17. Common Phrases and Expressions — 80
18. Telling Time — 86
19. Describing Weather — 91
20. Basic Verbs and Conjugation — 96
21. Present Tense Verbs — 102
22. Negation — 108
23. Introduction to Adjectives — 113

24. Comparisons and Superlatives	118
25. Food and Drinks	124
26. Shopping and Currency	130
27. Directions and Locations	136
28. Transportation	142
29. Health and Body Parts	148
30. Animals and Nature	153
31. School and Education	158
32. Work and Office Vocabulary	164
33. House and Home	171
34. Clothes and Fashion	176
35. Reflexive Verbs	182
36. Past Tense: Passé Composé	186
37. Past Tense: Imparfait	191
38. Future Tense	196
39. Conditional Mood	201
40. Subjunctive Mood	207
41. Prepositions	212
42. Conjunctions	218
43. Indirect and Direct Object Pronouns	223
44. Advanced Grammar Rules	227

Chapter 1

Introduction to French

Welcome to **Step-by-Step French: From Alphabet to Conversation**! We are so excited that you've decided to start learning French. Whether you're interested in French because it's spoken in many different countries, or because you want to be able to understand French movies, music, and books, you're in the right place. This book is designed to guide you through learning French, step by step, from the very basics all the way to having conversations. We've made sure that everything is clear, easy to follow, and fun, so you'll enjoy the journey as you become a French speaker.

Now, you might be wondering: **Why should I learn French?** Great question! French is one of the most widely spoken languages in the world. It's the official language in 29 countries, including France, Canada, Belgium, and many countries in Africa. It's also one of the official languages of international organizations like the United Nations and the European Union. But learning French isn't just about communication; it's also about culture. By learning French, you'll get a deeper understanding of French art, music, literature, and history. Plus, French is a Romance language, which means it shares a lot in common with other languages like Spanish, Italian, and Portuguese. So, learning French can make it easier to learn other languages in the future!

In this book, we'll start with the basics, because every great journey begins with a single step. You'll learn the **French Alphabet**, which is very similar to the English alphabet, with just a few differences. Once you're comfortable with the alphabet, we'll move on to **Pronunciation**. French pronunciation can seem tricky at first, but don't worry! We'll break it down for you so that you can practice and get it just right.

Next, we'll dive into some of the most important parts of any language: **Basic Greetings and Introductions**. You'll learn how to say "hello," "goodbye," and "how are you?" in French. For example, "hello" in French is bonjour (bohn-zhoor), and "goodbye" is au revoir (oh ruh-vwahr). These are phrases you'll use every day, so we'll make sure you know them well!

As we continue, you'll learn how to count in French with our chapter on **Numbers and Counting**. Numbers are everywhere, whether you're telling someone your age, asking for the time, or shopping. We'll help you learn to count from 1 to 100 and beyond, so you'll always be ready with the right number in French.

We'll also explore how to talk about **Days of the Week** and **Months and Seasons**. You'll learn how to say what day it is, plan something for the weekend, and talk about the different seasons. For example, "Monday" in French is lundi (lun-dee), and "winter" is l'hiver (lee-vair). Knowing how to talk about time is super important, and we'll make sure you're comfortable with these new words.

Colors are another fun topic, and we'll cover them in the chapter on **Colors**. Imagine being able to describe a beautiful sunset in French, or just telling someone your favorite color! "Red" in French is rouge (roozh), and "blue" is bleu (bluh). You'll learn all the colors of the rainbow and more.

Then, we'll move on to learning about the people around you with our chapter on **Family Members** and **Common Professions**. You'll learn how to say "mother," "father," "brother," and other family members in French. For example, "mother" is mère (mehr), and "father" is père (pehr). You'll also learn how to talk about what people do for work. "Teacher" in French is professeur (pro-fe-sseur), and "doctor" is docteur (dok-teur). These words will help you talk about your family and friends in French.

Now, learning a language isn't just about memorizing words. It's also about understanding **Basic Grammar Rules**. Don't worry, we've made this easy to follow! We'll start with **Articles and Gender**, because in French, every noun is either masculine or feminine. For example, the word for "book" is livre (leev-ruh), and it's masculine, so you say le livre (luh leev-ruh) for "the book." The word for "car" is voiture (vwah-tyoor), and it's feminine, so you say la voiture (lah vwah-tyoor) for "the car." Understanding gender in French is key to making your sentences sound right.

We'll also talk about **Singular and Plural Nouns**, so you can talk about one thing or many things. For example, "the cat" in French is le chat (luh shah), and "the cats" is les chats (lay shah). It's a small change, but it makes a big difference in what you're saying!

Next, we'll introduce **Subject Pronouns** like "I," "you," "he," "she," and so on. In French, "I" is je (zhuh), "you" (informal) is tu (tew), and "he" is il (eel). These pronouns are important because they tell who is doing the action in a sentence.

Then, we'll move on to **Possessive Adjectives** like "my," "your," and "his/her." For example, "my book" in French is mon livre (mohn leev-ruh), and "your car" is ta voiture (tah vwah-tyoor). Knowing these will help you talk about things that belong to you and others.

We'll also cover **Question Words**, which are super handy when you're trying to ask something. You'll learn how to say "who," "what," "where," "when," "why," and "how" in French. For example, "who" is qui (kee), and "what" is quoi (kwah). These words will help you get information and understand what others are asking you.

Once you've got the basics down, we'll introduce you to **Common Phrases and Expressions**. These are the kinds of things you'll hear and say all the time in everyday conversations. For example, "please" in French is s'il vous plaît (seel voo pleh), and "thank you" is merci (mehr-see). Learning these phrases will make you sound more natural and polite when speaking French.

We'll also teach you how to **Tell Time** in French, so you'll know how to ask and say what time it is. For example, "What time is it?" in French is Quelle heure est-il? (kel uhr ay teel), and "It's 3 o'clock" is Il est trois heures (eel ay trwa uhr). This is a useful skill for planning and being on time!

Talking about the weather is something people do all the time, so we'll show you how to **Describe Weather** in French. You'll learn phrases like "It's sunny" (Il fait du soleil - eel fay doo so-leyl) and "It's raining" (Il pleut - eel pleuh). This will help you chat about the weather with your French-speaking friends.

Finally, you'll learn about **Basic Verbs and Conjugation**. Verbs are action words, like "to eat," "to play," or "to learn." In French, verbs change depending on who is doing the action and when it's happening. For example, the verb "to eat" in French is manger (mahn-zhay), and you say je mange (zhuh mahnzh) for "I eat." We'll start with the **Present Tense**, which is used to talk about things that are happening right now. You'll learn how to use verbs in the present tense to make your sentences complete and meaningful.

Throughout the book, we've included lots of examples and practice exercises to help you reinforce what you've learned. Don't worry if you make mistakes—learning a new language is all about practice and improvement. By the time you finish this book, you'll have a strong foundation in French and the confidence to start using it in real-life situations.

So, let's get started on this exciting journey to learning French! Remember, every word you learn is a step closer to being able to speak, understand, and enjoy the French language. Bon voyage!

Chapter 2

The French Alphabet

Bienvenue! (Welcome!) In this chapter, we're going to start with the very first step of learning French: the French Alphabet. Just like in English, the French alphabet is the foundation for reading, writing, and speaking. Once you know the alphabet, you'll be able to pronounce words correctly and start building your French vocabulary. Don't worry if this is your first time learning a new alphabet—we'll go through each letter together, and by the end, you'll see that the French alphabet is not so different from the English one.

What is the French Alphabet?

The French alphabet has 26 letters, just like the English alphabet. Most of the letters look exactly the same, but there are a few differences in how they are pronounced. Learning the pronunciation is important because it helps you read and speak French correctly. Here's a quick look at the French alphabet:

A (ah), B (bay), C (say), D (day), E (uh), F (ef), G (zhay), H (ash), I (ee), J (zhee), K (kah), L (el), M (em), N (en), O (oh), P (pay), Q (koo), R (air), S (es), T (tay), U (oo), V (vay), W (doo-bluh-vay), X (eeks), Y (ee-grek), Z (zed)

Let's go through each letter one by one, with examples to help you remember.

A (ah): The letter A is pronounced like "ah," similar to the "a" in the English word "father." For example, the word ami (ah-mee), which means "friend," starts with the letter A.

B (bay): B is pronounced like "bay," just like the letter B in the English word "baby." An example in French is banane (bah-nan), which means "banana."

C (say): The letter C is pronounced "say." It's like the C in the English word "cat," but softer, especially when it comes before the letters e, i, or y. For example, cinéma (see-nay-mah) means "cinema."

D (day): D is pronounced "day," just like the D in the English word "dog." An example in French is dent (dahn), which means "tooth."

E (uh): The letter E is a little different. It's pronounced "uh," which is a bit like the sound in the English word "the." For example, école (ay-kohl) means "school."

F (ef): F is pronounced "ef," just like the F in the English word "fun." In French, fleur (flur) means "flower."

G (zhay): The letter G is pronounced "zhay." It's soft, like the G in the English word "beige." For example, gâteau (gah-toh), which means "cake," starts with a G.

H (ash): H is pronounced "ash." In French, the letter H is silent at the beginning of words, like in the word hôtel (oh-tel), which means "hotel."

I (ee): I is pronounced "ee," like the letter E in the English word "see." An example in French is île (eel), which means "island."

J (zhee): J is pronounced "zhee." It's like the sound in the English word "measure." For example, je (zhuh), which means "I," starts with a J.

K (kah): The letter K is pronounced "kah," just like in the English word "kite." However, K is not very common in French. An example is kiwi (kee-wee), which is the same as the English word "kiwi."

L (el): L is pronounced "el," like the L in the English word "lemon." In French, lune (loon), which means "moon," starts with an L.

M (em): M is pronounced "em," just like the M in the English word "mouse." For example, montagne (mohn-tahn), which means "mountain," starts with an M.

N (en): N is pronounced "en," just like the N in the English word "night." In French, nez (nay), which means "nose," starts with an N.

O (oh): The letter O is pronounced "oh," like the O in the English word "go." An example in French is orange (oh-rah-nzh), which means "orange" (the fruit or the color).

P (pay): P is pronounced "pay," just like the P in the English word "pen." In French, pomme (pohm), which means "apple," starts with a P.

Q (koo): The letter Q is pronounced "koo," like the Q in the English word "queue." In French, quatre (ka-truh), which means "four," starts with a Q.

R (air): R is pronounced "air," but with a rolled sound that's a bit tricky for English speakers. It's like the sound in the French word rouge (roozh), which means "red." Don't worry, with practice, you'll get the hang of it!

S (es): S is pronounced "es," just like the S in the English word "snake." In French, soleil (so-lay), which means "sun," starts with an S.

T (tay): The letter T is pronounced "tay," like the T in the English word "table." An example in French is téléphone (tay-lay-fohn), which means "telephone."

U (oo): U is a unique sound in French, pronounced "oo," but with your lips rounded more tightly than in English. It's like the sound in lune (loon), which means "moon." This might take some practice, but it's an important sound to learn!

V (vay): V is pronounced "vay," just like the V in the English word "violin." In French, voiture (vwah-tyoor), which means "car," starts with a V.

W (doo-bluh-vay): W is pronounced "doo-bluh-vay," which means "double V" in French. W is not very common in French, but you might see it in words like wagon (wah-gohn), which is the same as the English word "wagon."

X (eeks): X is pronounced "eeks," like the X in the English word "box." An example in French is taxi (tak-see), which means "taxi."

Y (ee-grek): Y is pronounced "ee-grek," which means "Greek I" in French. An example is yo-yo (yoh-yoh), which is the same in English and French.

Z (zed): Z is pronounced "zed," just like the Z in the English word "zebra." In French, zèbre (zeh-bruh), which also means "zebra," starts with a Z.

Accents in French

In addition to the 26 letters, the French language uses accents on some vowels. These accents change the pronunciation or meaning of words. Here are the main accents you'll see in French:

- **Accent aigu (é)**: This accent makes the "e" sound like "ay." For example, école (ay-kohl), which means "school."

- **Accent grave (è)**: This accent makes the "e" sound like "eh." For example, père (pehr), which means "father."

- **Accent circonflexe (ê)**: This accent can appear on any vowel and it usually doesn't change the pronunciation much, but it can change the meaning of a word. For example, forêt (foh-reh), which means "forest."

- **Tréma (ë)**: This accent is placed over a vowel to show that it should be pronounced separately. For example, Noël (noh-el), which means "Christmas."

- **Cédille (ç)**: This accent is placed under the letter C (ç) to make it sound like an "s." For example, français (frahn-say), which means "French."

Key Points to Remember:

1. **French Alphabet Basics:** The French alphabet has 26 letters, just like in English, but with different pronunciations for some letters, such as G (zhay) and R (air).

2. **Accents:** French uses several accents, like accent aigu (é), accent grave (è), accent circonflexe (ê), tréma (ë), and cédille (ç), which affect pronunciation and meaning.

3. **Pronunciation Tips:** Pay attention to unique French sounds, such as U (oo) with rounded lips, and practice rolling the R sound.

4. **Similarities to English:** Many French letters and sounds are similar to English, making it easier to learn with practice.

5. **Importance of Accents:** Accents can change both the pronunciation and meaning of words, so it's important to learn them alongside the alphabet.

Chapter 3

Pronunciation Guide

Now that you've learned the French alphabet, it's time to take the next step: understanding how to pronounce French words. French pronunciation might seem tricky at first, but with practice and patience, you'll get the hang of it. In this chapter, we'll go through the basics of French pronunciation, including vowels, consonants, and some special sounds that are unique to French. Let's dive in!

The Importance of Pronunciation

Pronunciation is all about how we say words. In French, just like in English, how you say a word can change its meaning. For example, in English, "read" can sound like "reed" (present tense) or "red" (past tense), depending on how you say it. In French, there are similar challenges, but don't worry! We'll go over everything you need to know so you can pronounce French words correctly and confidently.

Vowel Sounds

Let's start with vowels. In French, vowels are super important because they can sound different depending on whether they have an accent or where they appear in a word. Here's a breakdown of each vowel and how it's pronounced:

A (ah): The vowel "A" is pronounced "ah," similar to the "a" in the English word "father." For example, in the word ami (ah-mee), which means "friend," the "A" is pronounced just like that.

E (uh/ay): The letter "E" has a couple of different sounds depending on where it is in a word. If it's at the end of a word, it's often pronounced like "uh," as in le (luh), which means "the." But when it has an accent, like in école (ay-kohl), which means "school," it sounds more like "ay."

I (ee): The letter "I" is pronounced "ee," just like the "ee" in the English word "see." For example, in île (eel), which means "island," the "I" is pronounced this way.

O (oh): The vowel "O" is pronounced "oh," like the "o" in the English word "go." For instance, in the word orange (oh-rah-nzh), which means "orange," the "O" sounds like "oh."

U (oo): The letter "U" is pronounced "oo," but with a rounded mouth, making it sound different from the English "oo" in "moon." It's a unique sound in French, and it's found in words like lune (loon), which means "moon." Try saying "oo" while rounding your lips tightly—it might feel a bit strange at first, but you'll get used to it!

Y (ee/ee-grek): The letter "Y" is pronounced like "ee" when it appears in a word, similar to the "i" in "machine." For example, in style (steel), which means "style," the "Y" is pronounced this way. When you see it as a standalone letter, it's called i-grec (ee-grek), which means "Greek I."

Nasal Vowels

One of the unique features of French is nasal vowels. These are vowels that are pronounced with air flowing through the nose. They can be a bit challenging at first, but they give French its distinctive sound. Here are the main nasal vowels:

AN, AM, EN, EM: These combinations are pronounced like "ahng." For example, maman (mah-mahng), which means "mom," has a nasal sound.

IN, IM, EIN, AIM: These combinations are pronounced like "ang" with a bit of a nasal twang. For example, vin (vang), which means "wine," uses this nasal vowel.

ON, OM: These combinations are pronounced like "ohn," similar to the "on" in the English word "song," but with more nasal resonance. For example, nom (nohn), which means "name," uses this sound.

UN, UM: These combinations are pronounced like "uhng," with a nasal sound. For example, brun (bruhng), which means "brown," uses this nasal vowel.

Consonant Sounds

French consonants are similar to English consonants, but there are a few differences. Let's go over some of the key consonants:

C: The letter "C" is pronounced like "k" when it comes before "a," "o," or "u," as in carte (kart), which means "card." However, when "C" comes before "e" or "i," it's pronounced like "s," as in cinéma (see-nay-mah), which means "cinema."

G: The letter "G" is pronounced like "g" in "go" when it's followed by "a," "o," or "u," as in gâteau (gah-toh), which means "cake." When "G" is followed by "e" or "i," it's pronounced like "zh," as in génie (zhay-nee), which means "genius."

H: The letter "H" is always silent in French. This means you don't pronounce it at the beginning of words like hôtel (oh-tel), which means "hotel," or heure (uhr), which means "hour."

J: The letter "J" is pronounced like "zh," similar to the "s" in "measure." For example, je (zhuh), which means "I," is pronounced with this sound.

L: The letter "L" is pronounced like the "l" in "love." For example, lune (loon), which means "moon," uses this sound.

R: The French "R" is different from the English "R." It's pronounced at the back of the throat, almost like a soft growl. For example, in rouge (roozh), which means "red," the "R" is pronounced in this way. This might take some practice, but it's a key sound in French.

S: The letter "S" is pronounced like "s" in "see" when it's at the beginning of a word or between vowels, as in salut (sah-lew), which means "hi." However, when "S" is at the end of a word, it's usually silent, as in vous (voo), which means "you."

V: The letter "V" is pronounced like the "v" in "voice." For example, in vélo (vay-loh), which means "bike," the "V" sounds just like that.

W: The letter "W" is not very common in French, but when it does appear, it's usually pronounced like "v," as in wagon (vah-gohn), which means "wagon."

X: The letter "X" is pronounced like "ks," as in the English word "box." For example, taxi (tak-see), which means "taxi," uses this sound.

Z: The letter "Z" is pronounced like "z" in "zebra," as in the word zéro (zay-roh), which means "zero." However, just like with "S," when "Z" is at the end of a word, it's usually silent.

Special Sound Combinations

In French, there are some special combinations of letters that create unique sounds. Here are a few to keep in mind:

CH: The combination "CH" is pronounced like "sh," as in the word chat (shah), which means "cat."

GN: The combination "GN" is pronounced like the "ny" sound in the English word "canyon." For example, montagne (mohn-tahn), which means "mountain," uses this sound.

LL: The combination "LL" is usually pronounced like a single "l," but in some cases, it can sound like "y," especially in words like fille (fee-yuh), which means "girl."

QU: The combination "QU" is pronounced like "k," as in the word quatre (ka-truh), which means "four."

Silent Letters

One of the trickiest things about French pronunciation is the silent letters. In French, many words have letters at the end that you don't pronounce. For example:

- moi (mwah), which means "me"
- beaucoup (boh-koo), which means "a lot"
- chat (shah), which means "cat"

In all these words, the final letter or letters are silent. This is something you'll get used to with practice.

Key Points to Remember:

1. **French pronunciation is crucial** for speaking and understanding the language correctly, as it can change the meaning of words.

2. **Vowel sounds in French** can vary based on accents and position in a word, with unique pronunciations like "ah" for A, "uh/ay" for E, "ee" for I, "oh" for O, and "oo" for U.

3. **Nasal vowels** give French its distinctive sound, with combinations like AN, IN, ON, and UN pronounced through the nose.

4. **Consonants have specific rules**, such as silent "H," "C" sounding like "s" before "e" or "i," and "R" pronounced at the back of the throat.

5. **Special sound combinations** like CH (sh), GN (ny), and silent letters at the end of words are common in French pronunciation.

Chapter 4

Basic Greetings and Introductions

Bonjour! (Hello!) Now that you've learned the French alphabet and some basic pronunciation, it's time to start using what you know to have simple conversations. In this chapter, we're going to learn about **Basic Greetings and Introductions**. These are the first words and phrases you'll need when meeting people and starting a conversation in French. Let's dive in!

Greetings: Saying Hello and Goodbye

One of the first things you'll need to know when speaking French is how to say hello and goodbye. Let's start with "hello," which in French is bonjour (bohn-zhoor). You can use bonjour any time of the day when greeting someone. It's the most common way to say hello in French, and it's always polite.

Another way to greet someone, especially in the evening, is bonsoir (bohn-swahr), which means "good evening." You might use bonsoir after the sun goes down or when you arrive at an evening event.

When it's time to say goodbye, the most common phrase is au revoir (oh ruh-vwahr). This literally means "until we see each other again," but it's used just like "goodbye" in English. You can use au revoir in any situation.

If you're saying goodbye to someone you'll see soon, you can say à bientôt (ah byan-toh), which means "see you soon." And if you'll see them the next day, you can say à demain (ah duh-mahn), which means "see you tomorrow."

Here are a few more greetings and farewells you might find useful:

- Salut (sah-lew) - "Hi" or "Bye" (informal, used with friends or family)

- Bonne nuit (bohn nwee) - "Good night" (used when someone is going to bed)

- À tout à l'heure (ah toot ah luhr) - "See you later" (literally means "at the next hour")

Introducing Yourself

Now that you know how to greet people, it's important to know how to introduce yourself. When you meet someone for the first time, you'll want to tell them your name. The simplest way to do this is to say, Je m'appelle (zhuh mah-pel), followed by your name. This means "My name is…" For example, if your name is Emily, you would say, Je m'appelle Emily (zhuh mah-pel Emily).

Another way to introduce yourself is to say, Moi, c'est (mwah, say), followed by your name. This is a more informal way of saying "I'm…". For example, Moi, c'est John (mwah, say John) means "I'm John."

After introducing yourself, you might want to ask the other person's name. You can do this by saying, Comment tu t'appelles? (koh-mohn tew tah-pel), which means "What's your name?" If you're speaking to an adult or someone you don't know very well, it's more polite to say, Comment vous vous appelez? (koh-mohn voo voo zah-play), which is the formal version of the same question.

Here's a simple exchange to help you understand how this works:

- You: Bonjour! (Hello!)
- Them: Bonjour! (Hello!)
- You: Je m'appelle Sarah. (My name is Sarah.)
- Them: Moi, c'est Thomas. (I'm Thomas.)
- You: Enchanté(e). (Nice to meet you.)

Note: If you're a boy, you'll say Enchanté (ahn-shahn-tay), and if you're a girl, you'll add an extra "e" and say Enchantée (ahn-shahn-tay). Even though they sound the same, the spelling is different depending on whether you're male or female.

Asking How Someone Is

Once you've introduced yourself, it's polite to ask how the other person is doing. In French, you can ask this in a few different ways. The most common way is Comment ça va? (koh-mohn sah vah), which means "How's it going?" This is a friendly, casual way to ask someone how they are.

If you want to be a bit more formal or polite, you can ask, Comment allez-vous? (koh-mohn ah-lay voo), which means "How are you?" This is often used when speaking to someone you don't know very well or when you want to be extra polite.

You might also hear people simply say, Ça va? (sah vah), which is a very informal way of asking "Are you okay?" or "How's it going?" You can respond to any of these questions by saying:

- Ça va bien, merci. (sah vah byan, mehr-see) - "I'm doing well, thank you."

- Ça va mal. (sah vah mahl) - "I'm not doing well."

- Comme ci, comme ça. (kohm see, kohm sah) - "So-so."

After answering, it's polite to ask the same question back. You can do this by saying Et toi? (ay twah), which means "And you?" in an informal setting, or Et vous? (ay voo) if you want to be more formal.

Introducing Others

Sometimes, you might be in a situation where you need to introduce someone else. In French, you can introduce a friend or family member by saying, Voici (vwah-see), which means "Here is..." For example, if you're introducing your friend Sophie, you would say, Voici Sophie (vwah-see Sophie).

If you want to say, "This is...," you can use C'est (say). For example, C'est mon frère (say mohn frehr) means "This is my brother."

Here's a quick example of how you might introduce two friends:

- You: Voici Paul. (Here is Paul.)

- Friend 1: Enchanté, Paul. (Nice to meet you, Paul.)

- Friend 2: Enchanté(e). (Nice to meet you too.)

Remember, when introducing others, it's polite to wait for everyone to say Enchanté or Enchantée before moving on with the conversation.

Polite Phrases to Use

In French culture, being polite is very important. Here are some polite phrases you should know when having conversations:

- Merci (mehr-see) - "Thank you"

- Merci beaucoup (mehr-see boh-koo) - "Thank you very much"

- S'il vous plaît (seel voo pleh) - "Please" (formal)

- S'il te plaît (seel tuh pleh) - "Please" (informal)

- Pardon (par-dohn) - "Sorry" or "Excuse me"
- Excusez-moi (ehk-skew-zay mwah) - "Excuse me" (formal)
- De rien (duh ryen) - "You're welcome" (literally means "It's nothing")

These phrases are useful in many different situations, so it's good to practice them until they feel natural.

Other Useful Phrases

Here are a few more phrases that might come in handy when you're starting out with French:

- Oui (wee) - "Yes"
- Non (noh) - "No"
- D'accord (dah-kohr) - "Okay"
- Je ne sais pas (zhuh nuh say pah) - "I don't know"
- Je comprends (zhuh kom-prah) - "I understand"
- Je ne comprends pas (zhuh nuh kom-prah pah) - "I don't understand"
- Répétez, s'il vous plaît (ray-pay-tay, seel voo pleh) - "Please repeat that" (formal)
- Parlez-vous anglais? (par-lay voo ahn-glay) - "Do you speak English?"

Key Points to Remember:

1. **Basic Greetings:** Learn to greet people with bonjour (hello), bonsoir (good evening), and say goodbye with au revoir (goodbye) or à bientôt (see you soon).

2. **Introducing Yourself:** Introduce yourself by saying Je m'appelle (My name is…) followed by your name, and ask others their name with Comment tu t'appelles? (What's your name?).

3. **Asking How Someone Is:** Ask how someone is with Comment ça va? (How's it going?) or Comment allez-vous? (How are you?), and respond with Ça va bien, merci (I'm doing well, thank you).

4. **Polite Phrases:** Use polite expressions like Merci (Thank you), S'il vous plaît (Please, formal), Pardon (Sorry/Excuse me), and De rien (You're welcome).

5. **Other Useful Phrases:** Familiarize yourself with phrases like Oui (Yes), Non (No), Je ne sais pas (I don't know), and Répétez, s'il vous plaît (Please repeat that).

Chapter 5

Numbers and Counting

In this chapter, we're going to learn all about **Numbers and Counting** in French. Numbers are an essential part of any language because they help us talk about age, time, dates, quantities, and much more. By the end of this chapter, you'll be able to count in French, understand how numbers are used, and even start talking about things like your age or how many pets you have. Let's get started!

Counting from 1 to 10

Let's start with the basics: counting from 1 to 10. These are the first numbers you'll need to learn, and they're used all the time. Here's how you say them in French:

1 - un (uhng)

2 - deux (duh)

3 - trois (trwah)

4 - quatre (ka-truh)

5 - cinq (sank)

6 - six (sees)

7 - sept (set)

8 - huit (weet)

9 - neuf (nuhf)

10 - dix (dees)

Notice that some of these numbers, like un (uhng) and huit (weet), sound quite different from their English equivalents. Don't worry if they seem tricky at first; with a bit of practice, you'll get the hang of them.

Counting from 11 to 20

Once you're comfortable with the numbers 1 to 10, it's time to move on to 11 through 20. Here's how you say them in French:

11 - onze (ohnz)

12 - douze (dooz)

13 - treize (trehz)

14 - quatorze (ka-tohrz)

15 - quinze (kanz)

16 - seize (sez)

17 - dix-sept (dees-set)

18 - dix-huit (dees-weet)

19 - dix-neuf (dees-nuhf)

20 - vingt (van)

Just like in English, the numbers 11 to 16 each have their own unique names, but starting from 17, French numbers are formed by combining the word for 10 (dix) with the numbers 7, 8, and 9. This pattern makes it easier to remember them as you count higher.

Counting from 21 to 69

Now that you've mastered the numbers up to 20, let's keep going! In French, the numbers from 21 to 69 follow a pattern that's similar to English, but with a few differences:

21 - vingt et un (van tay uhng)

22 - vingt-deux (van duh)

23 - vingt-trois (van trwah)

24 - vingt-quatre (van ka-truh)

25 - vingt-cinq (van sank)

26 - vingt-six (van sees)

27 - vingt-sept (van set)

28 - vingt-huit (van weet)

29 - vingt-neuf (van nuhf)

30 - trente (tront)

Once you get to 30, the pattern repeats with the tens digit followed by the ones digit. Here are a few examples:

31 - trente et un (tront ay uhng)

32 - trente-deux (tront duh)

40 - quarante (ka-ront)

50 - cinquante (san-kont)

60 - soixante (swah-sont)

One thing to notice is that unlike in English, where we say "twenty-one" and "thirty-two," in French, you sometimes need to add an "et" (and) between the tens and ones digits, like in vingt et un (21) and trente et un (31).

Counting from 70 to 99

When you get to 70, French numbers start to get a little different from English. Instead of having a completely new word for 70, the French combine the words for 60 and 10 to make soixante-dix (swah-sont dees), which literally means "sixty-ten." Here's how it works:

70 - soixante-dix (swah-sont dees)

71 - soixante et onze (swah-sont ay ohnz)

72 - soixante-douze (swah-sont dooz)

73 - soixante-treize (swah-sont trehz)

80 - quatre-vingts (ka-truh van)

For 80, instead of a new word, the French say quatre-vingts, which literally means "four twenties." This might seem strange, but it's just how the French count! Here's how you continue:

81 - quatre-vingt-un (ka-truh van uhng)

82 - quatre-vingt-deux (ka-truh van duh)

90 - quatre-vingt-dix (ka-truh van dees)

When you reach 90, you combine 80 and 10 to get quatre-vingt-dix, which literally means "four twenties and ten." Here's how to count from 90 to 99:

91 - quatre-vingt-onze (ka-truh van ohnz)

92 - quatre-vingt-douze (ka-truh van dooz)

99 - quatre-vingt-dix-neuf (ka-truh van dees nuhf)

Once you've got these numbers down, you can count all the way to 99!

Counting to 100 and Beyond

Finally, we get to 100, which is cent (sahn) in French. Counting beyond 100 is just a matter of adding the other numbers you've learned:

101 - cent un (sahn uhng)

102 - cent deux (sahn duh)

150 - cent cinquante (sahn sank-ont)

200 - deux cents (duh sahn)

As you can see, counting in French follows a pattern, just like in English. Once you've learned the basic numbers, you can easily count to 100 and beyond!

Using Numbers in Everyday Life

Now that you know how to count in French, let's talk about how you can use these numbers in everyday situations. Here are some common ways to use numbers:

Talking about Age

When you want to tell someone how old you are, you can say, J'ai (zhay), followed by your age and the word ans (ahns), which means "years." For example:

"I am 12 years old" - J'ai douze ans (zhay dooz ah ns)

Telling Time

Numbers are also important when telling time. For example, to say "It's 3 o'clock," you would say Il est trois heures (eel ay trwah zuhr). Here's how you might say different times:

"It's 1 o'clock" - Il est une heure (eel ay oon zuhr)

"It's 2:30" - Il est deux heures et demie (eel ay duh zuhr ay duh-mee)

Talking about Quantities

Numbers are also used when talking about quantities. For example, if you're at a bakery and want to buy three croissants, you would say:

"I would like three croissants" - Je voudrais trois croissants (zhuh voo-dray trwah krwah-sahn)

Or if you're at a store and need to buy two apples, you could say:

"I'll take two apples" - Je prends deux pommes (zhuh prahn duh pohm)

Describing Things

Numbers can also be used to describe things, like how many pets you have, how many people are in your family, or how many books you have in your backpack. Here are some examples:

"I have one dog" - J'ai un chien (zhay uhng shee-ehn)

"There are four people in my family" - Il y a quatre personnes dans ma famille (eel yah ka-truh pair-sohn dahn mah fah-mee)

"I have six books in my backpack" - J'ai six livres dans mon sac à dos (zhay sees leevr dahn mohn sak ah doh)

Key Points to Remember:

1. **Basic Numbers:** Learn to count from 1 to 10 in French: un (1), deux (2), trois (3), quatre (4), cinq (5), six (6), sept (7), huit (8), neuf (9), dix (10).

2. **Patterns in Counting:** Numbers 11-16 have unique names, while 17-99 follow patterns, combining tens with units (e.g., dix-sept for 17, soixante-dix for 70, quatre-vingt for 80).

3. **Using Numbers Beyond 100:** The number 100 is cent, and you can continue counting by adding other numbers (e.g., cent un for 101, deux cents for 200).

4. **Talking About Age and Time:** Use numbers to talk about age (J'ai douze ans - I am 12 years old) and time (Il est trois heures - It's 3 o'clock).

5. **Practical Use of Numbers:** Use numbers in daily life for quantities and descriptions (e.g., Je voudrais trois croissants - I would like three croissants, J'ai un chien - I have one dog).

Chapter 6

Days of the Week

In this chapter, we're going to learn about the **Days of the Week** in French. Knowing the days of the week is essential because it helps you talk about your schedule, make plans, and understand when things are happening. By the end of this chapter, you'll be able to name all the days of the week in French, ask and answer questions about what day it is, and talk about your weekly activities. Let's get started!

The Days of the Week in French

Just like in English, there are seven days in the French week. Here's how you say each one:

Lundi (lun-dee) - Monday

Mardi (mar-dee) - Tuesday

Mercredi (mehr-kruh-dee) - Wednesday

Jeudi (zhuh-dee) - Thursday

Vendredi (vahn-druh-dee) - Friday

Samedi (sam-dee) - Saturday

Dimanche (dee-mahnsh) - Sunday

Notice that each day of the week in French ends with "-di" except for Sunday, which ends with "-anche." This can help you remember the days more easily.

Pronunciation Tips

Pronunciation is important when learning the days of the week in French. Here are some tips to help you say them correctly:

- **Lundi**: The "lun" part sounds like "lun" in "lunar," and the "di" is pronounced like "dee." So, lundi (lun-dee).

- **Mardi**: The "mar" sounds like "mar" in "martian," and the "di" is the same as in lundi. So, mardi (mar-dee).

- **Mercredi**: The "mer" sounds like "mare," the "cre" sounds like "creh," and the "di" is "dee." So, mercredi (mehr-kruh-dee).

- **Jeudi**: The "jeu" sounds like "zhuh," and the "di" is "dee." So, jeudi (zhuh-dee).

- **Vendredi**: The "ven" sounds like "vahn," the "dre" sounds like "druh," and the "di" is "dee." So, vendredi (vahn-druh-dee).

- **Samedi**: The "sam" sounds like "sam," and the "di" is "dee." So, samedi (sam-dee).

- **Dimanche**: The "di" is "dee," and the "manche" sounds like "mahnsh." So, dimanche (dee-mahnsh).

How to Use the Days of the Week

Now that you know the names of the days, let's talk about how to use them in sentences. In French, you can talk about what you do on certain days by using the phrase le (luh) before the day of the week. For example:

Le lundi, je vais à l'école. (luh lun-dee, zhuh vay ah lay-kohl) - On Mondays, I go to school.

Le mercredi, je joue au football. (luh mehr-kruh-dee, zhuh zhoo oh foot-bol) - On Wednesdays, I play soccer.

If you want to talk about something happening on a specific day (just once, not every week), you can say ce (suh) before the day. For example:

Ce samedi, je vais au cinéma. (suh sam-dee, zhuh vay oh see-nay-mah) - This Saturday, I'm going to the movies.

To ask someone what day it is, you can say:

Quel jour est-ce? (kel zhoor es) - What day is it?

To answer, you simply say, C'est (say), followed by the day:

C'est lundi. (say lun-dee) - It's Monday.

Talking About Your Week

Now that you know how to say the days of the week, you can start talking about your weekly routine in French. Let's look at some examples:

Lundi, you might say:

Le lundi, je vais à l'école à huit heures. (luh lun-dee, zhuh vay ah lay-kohl ah weet uhr) - On Mondays, I go to school at 8 o'clock.

Mardi, you could say:

Le mardi, j'ai un cours de danse après l'école. (luh mar-dee, zhay uh koor duh dahns ah-pray lay-kohl) - On Tuesdays, I have a dance class after school.

Mercredi, maybe:

Le mercredi, je ne vais pas à l'école. (luh mehr-kruh-dee, zhuh nuh vay pah ah lay-kohl) - On Wednesdays, I don't go to school.

Jeudi, perhaps:

Le jeudi, je fais mes devoirs l'après-midi. (luh zhuh-dee, zhuh fay may duh-vwahr lah-pray-mee-dee) - On Thursdays, I do my homework in the afternoon.

Vendredi, you might say:

Le vendredi, je regarde un film avec ma famille. (luh vahn-druh-dee, zhuh ruh-gard uhn film ah-vek mah fah-mee) - On Fridays, I watch a movie with my family.

Samedi, you could say:

Le samedi, je joue avec mes amis. (luh sam-dee, zhuh zhoo ah-vek may zah-mee) - On Saturdays, I play with my friends.

Dimanche, maybe:

Le dimanche, je me repose. (luh dee-mahnsh, zhuh muh ruh-pohz) - On Sundays, I rest.

These sentences help you describe what you do on different days of the week. You can change the activities to match your own routine.

Asking About and Planning Activities

When making plans with friends or talking about activities, you can use the days of the week to ask and answer questions. Here are some examples:

To ask when something is happening, you can say:

Quand est-ce que tu vas au parc? (kohn es kuh tew vah oh par-k) - When are you going to the park?

To answer, you could say:

Je vais au parc samedi. (zhuh vay oh par-k sam-dee) - I'm going to the park on Saturday.

If you want to invite someone to do something with you, you can say:

Veux-tu venir chez moi vendredi? (vuh tew vuh-neer shay mwah vahn-druh-dee) - Do you want to come to my house on Friday?

And to accept or decline an invitation, you could say:

Oui, je veux bien! (wee, zhuh vuh byan) - Yes, I'd like to!

Désolé(e), je ne peux pas samedi. (day-zoh-lay, zhuh nuh puh pah sam-dee) - Sorry, I can't on Saturday.

These phrases will help you make plans and talk about your schedule with friends and family.

Special Days and Holidays

In addition to the regular days of the week, there are also special days and holidays that are important to know. Here are a few examples:

La fête nationale (lah fet nah-syo-nal) - National Day (like the 4th of July in the USA, but it's July 14th in France)

Noël (noh-el) - Christmas

Le Nouvel An (luh noo-vel ahn) - New Year's Day

Pâques (pahk) - Easter

You can use the days of the week to talk about when these holidays happen. For example:

Noël est un mardi cette année. (noh-el eh uhn mar-dee set ah-nay) - Christmas is on a Tuesday this year.

Or:

Le Nouvel An tombe un dimanche. (luh noo-vel ahn tohm uhn dee-mahnsh) - New Year's Day falls on a Sunday.

Talking about special days like this helps you connect the days of the week to important events and celebrations.

Key Points to Remember:

1. **Days of the Week:** The seven days in French are lundi (Monday), mardi (Tuesday), mercredi (Wednesday), jeudi (Thursday), vendredi (Friday), samedi (Saturday), and dimanche (Sunday).

2. **Using Days in Sentences:** To talk about recurring events, use le (luh) before the day (e.g., Le lundi, je vais à l'école - On Mondays, I go to school). For one-time events, use ce (suh) before the day (e.g., Ce samedi, je vais au cinéma - This Saturday, I'm going to the movies).

3. **Asking and Answering Questions:** To ask about the day, use Quel jour est-ce? (What day is it?), and to answer, use C'est followed by the day (e.g., C'est lundi - It's Monday).

4. **Describing Weekly Activities:** Use the days of the week to describe your routine, like Le mercredi, je joue au football (On Wednesdays, I play soccer).

5. **Special Days and Holidays:** Connect the days of the week to special events, such as Noël (Christmas) and Le Nouvel An (New Year's Day).

Chapter 7

Months and Seasons

In this chapter, we're going to learn about **Months and Seasons** in French. Knowing the months and seasons is important because it helps you talk about the date, your birthday, holidays, and the different times of the year. By the end of this chapter, you'll be able to name all the months and seasons in French, ask and answer questions about when things happen, and describe the weather during different seasons. Let's get started!

The Months of the Year in French

Just like in English, there are 12 months in the French year. Here's how you say each one:

Janvier (zhahn-vyay) - January

Février (fay-vree-yay) - February

Mars (mars) - March

Avril (ah-vreel) - April

Mai (may) - May

Juin (zhwan) - June

Juillet (jwee-yay) - July

Août (oot) - August

Septembre (sep-tahmbr) - September

Octobre (ok-tohbr) - October

Novembre (noh-vahmbr) - November

Décembre (day-sahmbr) - December

As you can see, many of the French months look similar to their English counterparts, which makes them easier to remember. Let's go over some pronunciation tips to help you say them correctly.

Pronunciation Tips

- **Janvier**: The "Jan" part sounds like "zhahn," and the "vier" is like "v-yay." So, janvier (zhahn-vyay).

- **Février**: The "fé" sounds like "fay," and the "vrier" is like "vree-yay." So, février (fay-vree-yay).

- **Mars**: This one is straightforward, sounding just like "mars" in English, but with a slightly rolled "r" in French. So, mars (mars).

- **Avril**: The "Av" sounds like "ahv," and the "ril" is like "reel." So, avril (ah-vreel).

- **Mai**: This is pronounced like "may," just like in English. So, mai (may).

- **Juin**: The "ju" sounds like "zhw," and the "in" is nasal, sounding like "ahn." So, juin (zhwan).

- **Juillet**: The "ju" is like "zhw," and the "illet" sounds like "ee-yay." So, juillet (jwee-yay).

- **Août**: This one is a bit tricky. The "août" is pronounced like "oot." So, août (oot).

- **Septembre**: This is similar to English but with a French accent. So, septembre (sep-tahmbr).

- **Octobre**: Again, similar to English. So, octobre (ok-tohbr).

- **Novembre**: Also similar to English. So, novembre (noh-vahmbr).

- **Décembre**: The "dé" sounds like "day," and the "cembre" is like "sahmbr." So, décembre (day-sahmbr).

How to Use the Months in Sentences

Now that you know the names of the months, let's talk about how to use them in sentences. In French, you can talk about when something happens by using the word en (ahn) before the month. For example:

Je suis né en janvier. (zhuh swee nay ahn zhahn-vyay) - I was born in January.

Nous partons en vacances en juillet. (noo par-ton ahn vah-kahns ahn jwee-yay) - We go on vacation in July.

If you want to ask when something is happening, you can say:

Quand est ton anniversaire? (kahn eh ton ah-nee-ver-sair) - When is your birthday?

To answer, you could say:

Mon anniversaire est en octobre. (mohn ah-nee-ver-sair eh ahn ok-tohbr) - My birthday is in October.

These phrases will help you talk about important dates and events in French.

The Seasons in French

Just like the months, there are four seasons in French. Here's how you say them:

Le printemps (luh pran-tahn) - Spring

L'été (lay-tay) - Summer

L'automne (loh-ton) - Autumn/Fall

L'hiver (lee-vair) - Winter

Notice that the word for "season" in French is saison (say -sawn), and each season is used with the article "le" (luh) or "l'" (when the next word starts with a vowel or silent h). Let's break down the pronunciation and usage for each season:

Pronunciation Tips

- **Le printemps**: The "prin" sounds like "pran," and the "temps" is pronounced "tahn" with a nasal sound. So, le printemps (luh pran-tahn).

- **L'été**: The "é" sounds like "ay," and "té" also sounds like "tay." So, l'été (lay-tay).

- **L'automne**: The "au" sounds like "oh," and "tonne" sounds like "ton." So, l'automne (loh-ton).

- **L'hiver**: The "hi" sounds like "lee," and "ver" is pronounced "vair." So, l'hiver (lee-vair).

Talking About the Seasons

In French, you can talk about what happens during each season using the word en (ahn) for "in" or "during," just like with the months. For example:

En été, il fait chaud. (ahn lay-tay, eel fay show) - In summer, it's hot.

En hiver, il neige. (ahn lee-vair, eel nehj) - In winter, it snows.

You can also talk about your favorite season by saying:

Ma saison préférée est l'automne. (mah say-zon pray-fay-ray eh loh-ton) - My favorite season is autumn.

To ask someone about their favorite season, you could say:

Quelle est ta saison préférée? (kel eh tah say-zon pray-fay-ray) - What is your favorite season?

Describing the Weather in Each Season

Each season has different weather, and you can describe the weather using some basic phrases. Here are a few examples for each season:

Le printemps:

En printemps, il pleut souvent. (ahn pran-tahn, eel pleuh soo-vahn) - In spring, it rains often.

Les fleurs commencent à pousser. (lay flur koh-mohns ah poo-say) - The flowers start to grow.

L'été:

En été, il fait très chaud. (ahn lay-tay, eel fay tray show) - In summer, it's very hot.

Nous allons à la plage. (noo ah-lon ah lah plahzh) - We go to the beach.

L'automne:

En automne, les feuilles tombent. (ahn loh-ton, lay fuhy tohm) - In autumn, the leaves fall.

Il fait frais et venteux. (eel fay freh ay von-tuh) - It's cool and windy.

L'hiver:

En hiver, il neige souvent. (ahn lee-vair, eel nehj soo-vahn) - In winter, it snows often.

Nous faisons du ski. (noo fay-zon dew skee) - We go skiing.

These phrases help you describe what each season is like in French and talk about activities you might do during each season.

Special Days in Each Season

Just like in English, there are special holidays and events associated with each season. Here are a few examples:

Le printemps:

Pâques (pahk) - Easter, which usually happens in April.

La Fête du Travail (lah fet dew tra-vahy) - Labor Day, celebrated on May 1st in France.

L'été:

La Fête Nationale (lah fet nah-syo-nal) - Bastille Day, celebrated on July 14th.

Les grandes vacances (lay grahnd vah-kahns) - Summer vacation, which lasts from July to early September.

L'automne:

La Toussaint (lah too-sanh) - All Saints' Day, celebrated on November 1st.

La rentrée (lah rahn-tray) - Back to school in September.

L'hiver:

Noël (noh-el) - Christmas, celebrated on December 25th.

Le Nouvel An (luh noo-vel ahn) - New Year's Day, celebrated on January 1st.

You can use the months and seasons to talk about when these special days happen. For example:

Noël est en décembre. (noh-el eh ahn day-sahmbr) - Christmas is in December.

La Fête Nationale est en été. (lah fet nah-syo-nal eh ahn lay-tay) - Bastille Day is in summer.

Key Points to Remember:

1. **Months of the Year:** Learn the 12 months in French, such as janvier (January), février (February), and décembre (December). These are crucial for discussing dates and events.

2. **Seasons in French:** The four seasons are le printemps (spring), l'été (summer),

l'automne (autumn), and l'hiver (winter). Knowing these helps you describe the time of year.

3. **Using 'En' for Dates:** Use en before months and seasons to talk about when something happens, like en janvier (in January) or en été (in summer).

4. **Describing Weather:** Each season has its typical weather, such as il fait chaud (it's hot) in summer and il neige (it snows) in winter. These descriptions are useful for talking about seasonal activities.

5. **Special Days and Holidays:** Different seasons have special days, like Noël (Christmas) in winter and La Fête Nationale (Bastille Day) in summer, which are tied to specific months and seasons.

Chapter 8

Colors

In this chapter, we're going to learn about **Colors** in French. Colors are a fun and essential part of language because they help you describe the world around you. By the end of this chapter, you'll know how to name different colors in French, use them in sentences, and even describe things you see every day. Let's jump into the colorful world of French!

Basic Colors in French

Let's start by learning the names of some basic colors in French. Here are the most common ones:

Rouge (roozh) - Red

Bleu (bluh) - Blue

Jaune (zhon) - Yellow

Vert (vehr) - Green

Noir (nwar) - Black

Blanc (blahn) - White

Orange (oh-rahnzh) - Orange

Rose (rohz) - Pink

Violet (vee-oh-lay) - Purple

Marron (mah-rohn) - Brown

Gris (gree) - Gray

These are the basic colors that you'll use most often when describing things. Let's go over some pronunciation tips to help you say them correctly.

Pronunciation Tips

- **Rouge**: The "rou" sounds like "roo," and the "ge" sounds like "zh" in "treasure." So, rouge (roozh).

- **Bleu**: The "bleu" is pronounced like "bluh," with a short, soft sound. So, bleu (bluh).

- **Jaune**: The "j" sounds like "zh" in "measure," and the "aune" is like "ohn." So, jaune (zhon).

- **Vert**: The "v" is like in English, and "ert" sounds like "air" but with a slightly rolled "r." So, vert (vehr).

- **Noir**: The "no" is like "noh," and "ir" is like "war." So, noir (nwar).

- **Blanc**: The "bl" sounds like "blah," and the "anc" is like "ahn." So, blanc (blahn).

- **Orange**: This word is similar to English but with a French twist. The "o" is like "oh," and "range" is like "rahnzh." So, orange (oh-rahnzh).

- **Rose**: The "r" is rolled, and "ose" sounds like "ohz." So, rose (rohz).

- **Violet**: The "vio" is like "vee-oh," and "let" is like "lay." So, violet (vee-oh-lay).

- **Marron**: The "mar" is like "mahr," and "ron" is like "rohn." So, marron (mah-rohn).

- **Gris**: The "g" is like "gr" in "green," and "is" is like "ee." So, gris (gree).

Using Colors in Sentences

Now that you know the names of the colors, let's talk about how to use them in sentences. In French, colors are adjectives, which means they describe nouns. When using colors in a sentence, they usually come after the noun they describe. Here's an example:

La pomme est rouge. (lah pohm eh roozh) - The apple is red.

Notice how rouge (red) comes after pomme (apple). This is different from English, where the color usually comes before the noun.

Here's another example:

Le ciel est bleu. (luh syel eh bluh) - The sky is blue.

Again, the color bleu (blue) comes after the noun ciel (sky).

Gender and Number Agreement

In French, adjectives, including colors, must agree with the noun they describe in gender (masculine or feminine) and number (singular or plural). This means that the form of the color might change depending on the noun. Let's look at some examples:

Le chat noir (luh shah nwar) - The black cat (masculine, singular)

La voiture noire (lah vwah-tyoor nwar) - The black car (feminine, singular)

Les chats noirs (lay shah nwar) - The black cats (masculine, plural)

Les voitures noires (lay vwah-tyoor nwar) - The black cars (feminine, plural)

As you can see, the color noir (black) changes to noire when it describes a feminine noun, and it adds an "s" at the end when the noun is plural. However, in spoken French, you might not always hear the difference because the pronunciation often stays the same.

Describing Things with Colors

Now that you know how to use colors in sentences, let's practice describing different things around you. Here are some examples:

Le livre est bleu. (luh leevr eh bluh) - The book is blue.

La fleur est jaune. (lah flur eh zhon) - The flower is yellow.

Les maisons sont blanches. (lay may-zon sohn blahnsh) - The houses are white.

La chaise est verte. (lah shez eh vehrt) - The chair is green.

You can use these sentences to describe almost anything you see, from your clothes to the things in your classroom or home.

Mixing Colors

Just like in English, you can also talk about different shades and combinations of colors in French. Here are some examples:

Clair (klehr) - Light

Foncé (fohn-say) - Dark

You can use these words to create different shades of colors. For example:

Bleu clair (bluh klehr) - Light blue

Vert foncé (vehr fohn-say) - Dark green

You can also combine colors to describe something that has more than one color. For example:

Un t-shirt rouge et blanc (uhn tee-shurt roozh ay blahn) - A red and white t-shirt

Des chaussures marron et noir (day sho-sur mah-rohn ay nwar) - Brown and black shoes

Talking About Your Favorite Colors

Everyone has a favorite color, and in French, you can easily talk about yours. To say "My favorite color is…," you can say:

Ma couleur préférée est… (mah koo-luhr pray-fay-ray eh…)

For example:

Ma couleur préférée est le bleu. (mah koo-luhr pray-fay-ray eh luh bluh) - My favorite color is blue.

Ma couleur préférée est le rouge. (mah koo-luhr pray-fay-ray eh luh roozh) - My favorite color is red.

If you want to ask someone what their favorite color is, you can say:

Quelle est ta couleur préférée? (kel eh tah koo-luhr pray-fay-ray) - What is your favorite color?

And they might answer:

Ma couleur préférée est le vert. (mah koo-luhr pray-fay-ray eh luh vehr) - My favorite color is green.

Colors in Nature

Colors are all around us, especially in nature. Let's look at how you might describe different things in nature using the colors you've learned:

Le ciel est bleu. (luh syel eh bluh) - The sky is blue.

Les feuilles sont vertes. (lay fuhy sohn vehrt) - The leaves are green.

La mer est bleue. (lah mehr eh bluh) - The sea is blue.

Le soleil est jaune. (luh soh-lay eh zhon) - The sun is yellow.

Les montagnes sont marron. (lay mon-tahn sohn mah-rohn) - The mountains are brown.

These sentences show you how to use colors to describe the beautiful things you see outside.

Using Colors to Describe Clothes

You can also use colors to talk about what you're wearing or what others are wearing. Here are some examples:

Je porte un pantalon noir. (zhuh port uhn pahn-tah-lohn nwar) - I'm wearing black pants.

Elle porte une robe rouge. (el port oon rob roozh) - She's wearing a red dress.

Il a un chapeau bleu. (eel ah uhn shah-poh bluh) - He has a blue hat.

Ils portent des chaussures blanches. (eel port day sho-sur blahnsh) - They are wearing white shoes.

Talking about colors is a great way to describe your style and the things you see every day.

Key Points to Remember:

1. **Basic Colors:** Learn the names of common colors in French, such as rouge (red), bleu (blue), vert (green), and noir (black).

2. **Gender and Number Agreement:** Colors in French must agree with the gender and number of the nouns they describe, for example, le chat noir (the black cat, masculine) and la voiture noire (the black car, feminine).

3. **Using Colors in Sentences:** In French, color adjectives usually come after the noun, such as la pomme est rouge (the apple is red).

4. **Shades and Combinations:** You can describe shades by adding clair (light) or foncé (dark), like bleu clair (light blue) or vert foncé (dark green).

5. **Talking About Favorites:** To express your favorite color, use the phrase Ma couleur préférée est... (My favorite color is...), followed by the color.

Chapter 9

Family Members

In this chapter, we're going to learn about **Family Members** in French. Talking about your family is one of the most common conversations you'll have, whether you're introducing your family to someone or just talking about the people in your life. By the end of this chapter, you'll know how to name different family members in French, use them in sentences, and describe your own family. Let's begin!

Basic Family Members in French

Let's start with the most important family members. Here's how you say them in French:

La mère (lah mehr) - Mother

Le père (luh pehr) - Father

Le fils (luh fees) - Son

La fille (lah fee) - Daughter

Le frère (luh frehr) - Brother

La sœur (lah suhr) - Sister

Les parents (lay pah-rohn) - Parents

Les enfants (lay zahn-fahn) - Children

La grand-mère (lah grahn mehr) - Grandmother

Le grand-père (luh grahn pehr) - Grandfather

These are the basic terms you'll use to talk about your immediate family. Let's break down the pronunciation to make sure you can say them correctly.

Pronunciation Tips

- **La mère**: The "mère" sounds like "mehr," with a soft "r" at the end. So, la mère (lah mehr).

- **Le père**: The "père" is pronounced like "pehr," with a soft "r" as well. So, le père (luh pehr).

- **Le fils**: The "fils" sounds like "fees," even though the "l" and "s" are not pronounced separately. So, le fils (luh fees).

- **La fille**: The "fille" is pronounced like "fee-yuh." So, la fille (lah fee).

- **Le frère**: The "frère" sounds like "frehr," with a rolled "r." So, le frère (luh frehr).

- **La sœur**: The "sœur" sounds like "suhr," with the "r" rolled slightly. So, la sœur (lah suhr).

- **Les parents**: The "parents" sounds like "pah-rohn," with a nasal "on" sound. So, les parents (lay pah-rohn).

- **Les enfants**: The "enfants" sounds like "ahn-fahn," with both syllables nasalized. So, les enfants (lay zahn-fahn).

- **La grand-mère**: The "grand" sounds like "grahn," and "mère" is like "mehr." So, la grand-mère (lah grahn mehr).

- **Le grand-père**: The "grand" is "grahn," and "père" is "pehr." So, le grand-père (luh grahn pehr).

Extended Family Members

In addition to your immediate family, you might also want to talk about your extended family. Here are some more terms you can use:

L'oncle (lon-kluh) - Uncle

La tante (lah tahnt) - Aunt

Le cousin (luh koo-zan) - Male Cousin

La cousine (lah koo-zeen) - Female Cousin

Le neveu (luh nuh-vuh) - Nephew

La nièce (lah nee-ess) - Niece

These words will help you talk about your aunts, uncles, cousins, nephews, and nieces. Let's look at the pronunciation:

- **L'oncle**: The "oncle" sounds like "on-kluh," with a nasal "on" sound. So, l'oncle (lon-kluh).

- **La tante**: The "tante" sounds like "tahnt," with a short "a" sound. So, la tante (lah tahnt).

- **Le cousin**: The "cousin" is pronounced like "koo-zan," with a nasal "an" sound. So, le cousin (luh koo-zan).

- **La cousine**: The "cousine" sounds like "koo-zeen," with a soft "n." So, la cousine (lah koo-zeen).

- **Le neveu**: The "neveu" sounds like "nuh-vuh," with a soft "v." So, le neveu (luh nuh-vuh).

- **La nièce**: The "nièce" is pronounced like "nee-ess." So, la nièce (lah nee-ess).

Describing Your Family

Now that you know the names of your family members, let's talk about how to describe your family in French. You can use simple sentences to talk about who's in your family and what they're like. Here are some examples:

J'ai une grande famille. (zhay oon grahnd fah-mee) - I have a big family.

Ma mère s'appelle Claire. (mah mehr sah-pel Kler) - My mother's name is Claire.

Mon père est très gentil. (mohn pehr eh tray zhahn-tee) - My father is very kind.

J'ai un frère et deux sœurs. (zhay uhng frehr ay duh suhr) - I have one brother and two sisters.

Mes grands-parents habitent à Paris. (may grahn-par-rohn ah-beet ah pah-ree) - My grandparents live in Paris.

These sentences help you introduce your family members and talk about who they are. You can also describe what they do or what they like:

Mon frère aime jouer au football. (mohn frehr em zhoo-ay oh foot-bol) - My brother likes to play soccer.

Ma sœur adore lire des livres. (mah suhr ah-dor leer day leevr) - My sister loves to read books.

Ma tante est professeur. (mah tahnt eh pro-fes-seur) - My aunt is a teacher.

Mon oncle travaille dans un hôpital. (mohn lon-kluh tra-vahy dahn uhn oh-pee-tal) - My uncle works in a hospital.

Talking About Your Pets

In French, pets are often considered part of the family too. Here are some words you can use to talk about your pets:

Le chien (luh shyan) - Dog

Le chat (luh shah) - Cat

Le poisson (luh pwah-sohn) - Fish

L'oiseau (lwah-zoh) - Bird

Le lapin (luh lah-pan) - Rabbit

Here are some examples of how to talk about your pets:

J'ai un chien et deux chats. (zhay uhng shyan ay duh shah) - I have a dog and two cats.

Mon chien s'appelle Max. (mohn shyan sah-pel Max) - My dog's name is Max.

Mon chat est très mignon. (mohn shah eh tray meen-yohn) - My cat is very cute.

Nous avons un poisson rouge. (noo zah-von uhn pw ah-sohn roozh) - We have a goldfish.

Talking about your pets is a great way to share more about your family in French.

Using Possessive Adjectives

When talking about your family members, it's important to know how to use possessive adjectives in French. These are words like "my," "your," "his," and "her." Here's how you use them:

Mon (mohn) - My (used with masculine singular nouns)

Ma (mah) - My (used with feminine singular nouns)

Mes (may) - My (used with plural nouns)

Here are some examples:

Mon père est médecin. (mohn pehr eh may-dsin) - My father is a doctor.

Ma mère est infirmière. (mah mehr eh tan-firm-yair) - My mother is a nurse.

Mes parents sont très gentils. (may pah-rohn sohn tray zhahn-tee) - My parents are very kind.

These possessive adjectives change depending on whether the noun is masculine, feminine, or plural. Practice using them to talk about your own family members.

Asking About Someone's Family

To ask someone about their family in French, you can use these simple questions:

Tu as des frères et sœurs? (tew ah day frehr ay suhr) - Do you have any brothers and sisters?

Comment s'appelle ta mère? (koh-mohn sah-pel tah mehr) - What is your mother's name?

Il y a combien de personnes dans ta famille? (eel yah kohm-byen duh pair-sohn dahn tah fah-mee) - How many people are in your family?

These questions help you learn more about someone else's family and have a conversation about the people who are important to them.

Talking About Family Activities

You can also talk about what your family likes to do together. Here are some examples:

Nous aimons faire des promenades en famille. (noo eh-mohn fehr day pro-men-ahd ahn fah-mee) - We like to go on walks as a family.

Ma famille regarde des films le week-end. (mah fah-mee ruh-gard day film luh week-end) - My family watches movies on the weekend.

Le dimanche, nous mangeons ensemble. (luh dee-mahnsh, noo mahn-zhon ahn-sombl) - On Sundays, we eat together.

These sentences help you describe how you spend time with your family and what activities you enjoy doing together.

Key Points to Remember:

1. **Basic Family Members:** Learn the names of key family members in French, such as la mère (mother), le père (father), le frère (brother), and la sœur (sister).

2. **Extended Family:** Expand your vocabulary with terms for extended family, like l'oncle (uncle), la tante (aunt), le cousin (male cousin), and la cousine (female cousin).

3. **Describing Your Family:** Use simple sentences to describe your family members and what they do, e.g., Mon père est professeur (My father is a teacher).

4. **Talking About Pets:** Include pets in your family descriptions using words like le chien (dog) and le chat (cat).

5. **Possessive Adjectives:** Practice using mon (my, masculine), ma (my, feminine), and mes (my, plural) to talk about your family members.

Chapter 10

Common Professions

In this chapter, we're going to learn about **Common Professions** in French. Knowing how to talk about different jobs and professions is important because it helps you describe what people do and understand more about the world around you. By the end of this chapter, you'll be able to name various professions in French, use them in sentences, and ask and answer questions about what people do for work. Let's get started!

Basic Professions in French

Let's start by learning the names of some common professions. Here are a few that you might recognize:

Le médecin (luh mayd-sin) - Doctor

L'infirmier (lan-feer-myay) - Nurse (male)

L'infirmière (lan-feer-myair) - Nurse (female)

Le professeur (luh pro-fes-seur) - Teacher

L'avocat (lah-voh-kah) - Lawyer (male)

L'avocate (lah-voh-kat) - Lawyer (female)

Le policier (luh poh-lee-syay) - Police officer (male)

La policière (lah poh-lee-syair) - Police officer (female)

Le pompier (luh pom-pyay) - Firefighter

L'ingénieur (lan-zhen-yur) - Engineer

Le dentiste (luh don-teest) - Dentist

Le serveur (luh ser-vur) - Waiter

La serveuse (lah ser-vuhz) - Waitress

Le cuisinier (luh kwee-zee-nyay) - Cook (male)

La cuisinière (lah kwee-zee-nyair) - Cook (female)

These are just a few of the many professions you can learn in French. Let's go over some pronunciation tips to help you say them correctly.

Pronunciation Tips

- **Le médecin**: The "mé" sounds like "may," and "decin" is like "d-sin" with a soft "n." So, le médecin (luh mayd-sin).

- **L'infirmier**: The "in" is nasal, sounding like "an," and "firmier" is like "feer-myay." So, l'infirmier (lan-feer-myay).

- **L'infirmière**: Similar to "infirmier," but with a "myair" sound at the end. So, l'infirmière (lan-feer-myair).

- **Le professeur**: The "profes" is like "pro-fess," and "seur" is pronounced "sur." So, le professeur (luh pro-fes-seur).

- **L'avocat**: The "avo" is like "ah-vo," and "cat" sounds like "kah." So, l'avocat (lah-voh-kah).

- **L'avocate**: Similar to "avocat," but with a "kat" sound at the end. So, l'avocate (lah-voh-kat).

- **Le policier**: The "poli" is like "poh-lee," and "cier" sounds like "syay." So, le policier (luh poh-lee-syay).

- **La policière**: Similar to "policier," but with a "syair" sound at the end. So, la policière (lah poh-lee-syair).

- **Le pompier**: The "pom" sounds like "pohm," and "pier" is like "pyay." So, le pompier (luh pom-pyay).

- **L'ingénieur**: The "ingé" is like "an-zhay," and "nieur" sounds like "nyur." So, l'ingénieur (lan-zhen-yur).

- **Le dentiste**: The "dent" sounds like "dahn," and "iste" is like "eest." So, le dentiste (luh don-teest).

- **Le serveur**: The "serv" is like "ser," and "eur" sounds like "ur." So, le serveur (luh ser-vur).

- **La serveuse**: Similar to "serveur," but with a "vuhz" sound at the end. So, la serveuse (lah ser-vuhz).

- **Le cuisinier**: The "cui" is like "kwee," and "sinier" sounds like "zee-nyay." So, le cuisinier (luh kwee-zee-nyay).

- **La cuisinière**: Similar to "cuisinier," but with a "nyair" sound at the end. So, la cuisinière (lah kwee-zee-nyair).

Using Professions in Sentences

Now that you know some common professions, let's talk about how to use them in sentences. In French, you can say what someone does by using the verb être (to be) followed by the profession. Here are some examples:

Ma mère est infirmière. (mah mehr eh tan-feer-myair) - My mother is a nurse.

Mon père est professeur. (mohn pehr eh pro-fes-seur) - My father is a teacher.

Je veux devenir médecin. (zhuh vuh duh-vuh-neer mayd-sin) - I want to become a doctor.

Mon oncle est policier. (mohn lon-kluh eh poh-lee-syay) - My uncle is a police officer.

Notice how the profession comes after the verb être (to be) in each sentence. This is how you can describe what someone does for a living in French.

Asking About Someone's Job

If you want to ask someone what they do for work, you can use the question Qu'est-ce que tu fais dans la vie? (kes-kuh tew fay dahn lah vee), which means "What do you do for a living?"

To answer, you can say:

Je suis médecin. (zhuh swee mayd-sin) - I am a doctor.

Je travaille comme ingénieur. (zhuh trah-vay kom an-zhen-yur) - I work as an engineer.

If you want to ask someone else what they do, you can say:

Qu'est-ce que ton père fait dans la vie? (kes-kuh ton pehr fay dahn lah vee) - What does your father do for a living?

To answer, you might say:

Mon père est avocat. (mohn pehr eh lah-voh-kah) - My father is a lawyer.

These phrases will help you have conversations about jobs and professions in French.

Talking About Where People Work

In addition to knowing what people do, it's also useful to know where they work. Here are some places where people with different professions might work:

L'hôpital (loh-pee-tal) - Hospital

L'école (lay-kohl) - School

Le bureau (luh bew-roh) - Office

Le restaurant (luh res-toh-ron) - Restaurant

La caserne de pompiers (lah kah-zern duh pom-pyay) - Fire station

Le tribunal (luh tree-byu-nahl) - Courthouse

Here are some examples of how to use these places in sentences:

Ma mère travaille à l'hôpital. (mah mehr trah-vay ah loh-pee-tal) - My mother works at the hospital.

Mon père travaille dans un bureau. (mohn pehr trah-vay dahn uhn bew-roh) - My father works in an office.

Mon frère travaille dans un restaurant. (mohn frehr trah-vay dahn uhn res-toh-ron) - My brother works in a restaurant.

These sentences show you how to talk about where someone works in French.

Professions That Change Depending on Gender

In French, some professions have different forms depending on whether the person is male or female. You've already seen some examples like infirmier/infirmière (nurse) and avocat/avocate (lawyer). Here are a few more:

Le boulanger (luh boo-lahn-zhay) - Baker (male)

La boulangère (lah boo-lahn-zhehr) - Baker (female)

Le vendeur (luh vahn-duhr) - Salesperson (male)

La vendeuse (lah vahn-duhz) - Salesperson (female)

Le directeur (luh dee-rek-tuhr) - Director (male)

La directrice (lah dee-rek-trees) - Director (female)

When talking about someone's profession, it's important to use the correct form based on their gender. For example:

Ma mère est boulangère. (mah mehr eh boo-lahn-zhehr) - My mother is a baker.

Mon père est boulanger. (mohn pehr eh boo-lahn-zhay) - My father is a baker.

Talking About What You Want to Be

It's common to talk about what you want to be when you grow up. In French, you can say:

Je veux être... (zhuh vuh ehtr) - I want to be...

For example:

Je veux être médecin. (zhuh vuh ehtr mayd-sin) - I want to be a doctor.

Je veux être professeur. (zhuh vuh ehtr pro-fes-seur) - I want to be a teacher.

Je veux être ingénieur. (zhuh vuh ehtr an-zhen-yur) - I want to be an engineer.

You can use this phrase to talk about your dreams and goals for the future.

Key Points to Remember:

1. **Common Professions:** Learn the names of common professions in French, such as médecin (doctor), infirmier/infirmière (nurse), and professeur (teacher), and their gender variations.

2. **Using Professions in Sentences:** Use the verb être (to be) followed by a profession to describe what someone does, e.g., Je suis médecin (I am a doctor).

3. **Asking About Professions:** To ask someone about their job, use phrases like Qu'est-ce que tu fais dans la vie? (What do you do for a living?).

4. **Talking About Workplaces:** Learn to describe where someone works using places like l'hôpital (hospital) and le bureau (office).

5. **Gender Variations in Professions:** Some professions change based on gender, like boulanger/boulangère (baker), so it's important to use the correct form.

Chapter II

Basic Grammar Rules

In this chapter, we're going to explore some **Basic Grammar Rules** in French. Understanding grammar is like having a map that shows you how to put words together to make sentences. With these basic rules, you'll be able to start forming your own sentences in French, which is a big step towards becoming fluent. Let's dive in!

Subject Pronouns

First, let's talk about subject pronouns. Subject pronouns are words like "I," "you," "he," "she," and "they" in English. In French, these pronouns tell us who is doing the action in a sentence. Here are the French subject pronouns:

Je (zhuh) - I

Tu (tew) - You (informal)

Il (eel) - He

Elle (el) - She

Nous (noo) - We

Vous (voo) - You (formal or plural)

Ils (eel) - They (masculine or mixed group)

Elles (el) - They (feminine group)

Notice that je means "I" and is used when talking about yourself. Tu is informal and used when talking to a friend or someone your age, while vous is formal or plural, used when talking to an adult you don't know well or more than one person. Il and elle mean "he" and "she," and ils and elles are used for "they," with ils being for a group of males or a mixed group, and elles for a group of females.

Verb Conjugation in the Present Tense

Next, let's talk about verbs. Verbs are action words, like "to eat," "to play," or "to speak." In French, verbs change form depending on who is doing the action. This change is called conjugation. Let's look at the verb parler (par-lay), which means "to speak." Here's how it's conjugated in the present tense:

Je parle (zhuh parl) - I speak

Tu parles (tew parl) - You speak

Il/Elle parle (eel/el parl) - He/She speaks

Nous parlons (noo par-lon) - We speak

Vous parlez (voo par-lay) - You speak (formal/plural)

Ils/Elles parlent (eel/el parl) - They speak

Notice that the ending of the verb changes depending on the subject pronoun. For example, when je is the subject, the verb ends in "-e" (parle), and when nous is the subject, the verb ends in "-ons" (parlons). These endings are different for each subject pronoun and each verb type.

Negation

To make a sentence negative in French, you use the words ne (nuh) and pas (pah). These words go around the verb. For example, if you want to say "I don't speak," you would say:

Je ne parle pas. (zhuh nuh parl pah)

Here's how you would make other sentences negative:

Tu ne manges pas. (tew nuh mahnzh pah) - You don't eat.

Il ne joue pas. (eel nuh zhoo pah) - He doesn't play.

Nous ne regardons pas. (noo nuh ruh-gar-don pah) - We don't watch.

The words ne and pas work together to create the negative form, and they always go around the verb.

Articles and Gender

In French, every noun has a gender—it's either masculine or feminine. This gender affects the articles you use with the noun. The definite articles (which mean "the") are:

Le (luh) - for masculine singular nouns

La (lah) - for feminine singular nouns

L' (l) - used before a vowel or silent "h" (for both masculine and feminine singular nouns)

Les (lay) - for plural nouns

For example:

Le livre (luh leevr) - The book (masculine)

La chaise (lah shez) - The chair (feminine)

L'ami (lah-mee) - The friend (masculine, starting with a vowel)

Les enfants (lay zahn-fahn) - The children (plural)

It's important to remember the gender of each noun because it affects the article and sometimes even the adjective you use.

Singular and Plural Nouns

Just like in English, nouns in French can be singular (one) or plural (more than one). To make a noun plural, you usually add an "-s" at the end, but the pronunciation often stays the same. For example:

Un livre (uhn leevr) - A book

Des livres (day leevr) - Some books

Une pomme (oon pohm) - An apple

Des pommes (day pohm) - Some apples

Notice that the articles also change: un becomes des for masculine nouns, and une becomes des for feminine nouns when they are plural.

Adjective Agreement

In French, adjectives (words that describe nouns) must agree with the noun they describe in gender and number. This means that the form of the adjective might change depending on whether the noun is masculine, feminine, singular, or plural. Here's an example:

Un chat noir (uhn shah nwar) - A black cat (masculine, singular)

Une chaise noire (oon shez nwar) - A black chair (feminine, singular)

Des chats noirs (day shah nwar) - Some black cats (masculine, plural)

Des chaises noires (day shez nwahr) - Some black chairs (feminine, plural)

Notice how the adjective noir (black) changes to noire when describing a feminine noun and adds an "-s" when describing a plural noun.

Forming Questions

Asking questions in French can be done in several ways. One of the most common ways is by using est-ce que (es kuh) before a statement. For example, if you want to ask "Do you speak French?" you would say:

Est-ce que tu parles français? (es kuh tew parl frahn-say)

Another way to ask a question is to simply change the intonation of your voice at the end of a statement, similar to how we do in English. For example:

Tu parles français? (tew parl frahn-say) - You speak French?

You can also invert the subject and the verb to form a question, but this is a bit more formal. For example:

Parles-tu français? (parl tew frahn-say) - Do you speak French?

These different methods allow you to ask a variety of questions in French.

Possessive Adjectives

Possessive adjectives are words like "my," "your," "his," and "her" in English. In French, these words change depending on the gender and number of the noun they describe. Here are the French possessive adjectives:

Mon (mohn) - My (used with masculine singular nouns)

Ma (mah) - My (used with feminine singular nouns)

Mes (may) - My (used with plural nouns)

Here's how you can use them:

Mon livre (mohn leevr) - My book

Ma chaise (mah shez) - My chair

Mes livres (may leevr) - My books

It's important to use the correct possessive adjective based on the gender and number of the noun.

Demonstrative Adjectives

Demonstrative adjectives are used to point out specific things, like "this," "that," "these," and "those" in English. In French, the demonstrative adjectives are:

Ce (suh) - This/That (used with masculine singular nouns)

Cette (set) - This/That (used with feminine singular nouns)

Ces (say) - These/Those (used with plural nouns)

Here are some examples:

Ce livre (suh leevr) - This/That book

Cette chaise (set shez) - This/That chair

Ces livres (say leevr) - These/Those books

These adjectives help you specify which objects you're talking about in a conversation.

Key Points to Remember:

1. **Subject Pronouns and Verb Conjugation:** In French, subject pronouns like je (I), tu (you), il/elle (he/she), nous (we), and vous (you, formal/plural) guide verb conjugation in sentences.

2. **Negation:** To form a negative sentence, place ne before the verb and pas after it, as in Je ne parle pas (I don't speak).

3. **Gender and Articles:** Nouns have genders (masculine or feminine) that determine the articles le, la, un, une, and les, and affect adjective agreement.

4. **Plural Forms:** Most nouns become plural by adding an -s, but pronunciation often stays the same. Articles also change in the plural form, like un to des.

5. **Question Formation:** Questions can be asked using est-ce que, inversion (verb-subject order), or intonation, providing flexibility in conversation.

Chapter 12

Articles and Gender

In this chapter, we're going to explore an important part of French grammar: **Articles and Gender**. Understanding how articles and gender work in French is essential because they affect how you use nouns and adjectives. By the end of this chapter, you'll know how to use the correct articles with nouns, recognize the gender of nouns, and understand how this influences the rest of the sentence. Let's dive in!

What Are Articles?

Articles are small words that come before nouns. In English, the most common articles are "the," "a," and "an." French also has articles, but they work a little differently because they change depending on the gender and number of the noun. The two main types of articles in French are definite articles and indefinite articles.

Definite Articles

Definite articles are used when you're talking about a specific noun, similar to the English word "the." In French, the definite articles are:

Le (luh) - used with masculine singular nouns

La (lah) - used with feminine singular nouns

L' (l) - used with singular nouns that start with a vowel or silent "h" (both masculine and feminine)

Les (lay) - used with plural nouns (both masculine and feminine)

Here are some examples:

Le livre (luh leevr) - The book (masculine, singular)

La table (lah tah-bl) - The table (feminine, singular)

L'école (lay-kohl) - The school (feminine, singular, starts with a vowel)

Les enfants (lay zahn-fahn) - The children (plural)

Notice how the article changes depending on whether the noun is masculine or feminine, singular or plural. For nouns that start with a vowel, the article le or la becomes l' to make the sentence easier to say.

Indefinite Articles

Indefinite articles are used when you're talking about something unspecific or when you're introducing something for the first time, similar to "a" or "an" in English. In French, the indefinite articles are:

Un (uhn) - used with masculine singular nouns

Une (oon) - used with feminine singular nouns

Des (day) - used with plural nouns (both masculine and feminine)

Here are some examples:

Un livre (uhn leevr) - A book (masculine, singular)

Une table (oon tah-bl) - A table (feminine, singular)

Des livres (day leevr) - Some books (plural)

Des tables (day tah-bl) - Some tables (plural)

Just like with definite articles, the indefinite article changes based on the gender and number of the noun. It's important to remember these changes as you learn new words.

Understanding Gender in French

In French, every noun has a gender: it's either masculine or feminine. This might seem strange at first because in English, we don't think of objects as having gender. But in French, gender is an important part of the language. Knowing the gender of a noun helps you choose the right articles and adjectives to use with it.

Unfortunately, there aren't always clear rules for determining the gender of a noun, so it's something you'll need to memorize as you learn new words. However, there are some patterns that can help:

- Nouns that end in "-e" are often feminine, like la maison (lah meh-zon) - the house.

- Nouns that end in other letters are often masculine, like le livre (luh leevr) - the book.

- There are many exceptions to these patterns, so it's important to learn the gender with the noun as you go.

Let's look at some more examples:

Masculine Nouns

Le chien (luh shyan) - The dog

Un garçon (uhn gar-sohn) - A boy

Le cahier (luh kah-yay) - The notebook

Feminine Nouns

La fille (lah fee) - The girl

Une pomme (oon pohm) - An apple

La voiture (lah vwah-tyoor) - The car

As you can see, the article changes depending on whether the noun is masculine or feminine. This is why it's important to learn the gender of each noun as you study French.

Articles with Plural Nouns

When you're talking about more than one thing, you'll need to use the plural form of the noun and the appropriate article. In French, both masculine and feminine plural nouns use the same articles:

Les (lay) - The (used with plural nouns)

Des (day) - Some (used with plural nouns)

Here are some examples:

Les chiens (lay shyan) - The dogs

Des filles (day fee) - Some girls

Les voitures (lay vwah-tyoor) - The cars

Des pommes (day pohm) - Some apples

Notice how the article les is used with both masculine and feminine plural nouns, and the same goes for des. This makes it a little easier when talking about more than one thing.

Elision and Liaison

French has two important pronunciation rules that affect how articles are used: **elision** and **liaison**.

Elision occurs when the article le or la becomes l' before a noun that starts with a vowel or a silent "h." This makes the sentence flow more smoothly. For example:

L'école (lay-kohl) - The school (instead of la école)

L'ami (lah-mee) - The friend (masculine) (instead of le ami)

This elision helps avoid awkward pauses in speech and makes the language sound more fluid.

Liaison happens when the final consonant of a word is pronounced because the next word starts with a vowel. This often occurs with articles and nouns. For example:

Les amis (lay zah-mee) - The friends

Des enfants (day zahn-fahn) - Some children

In these examples, the "s" at the end of les and des is normally silent, but it's pronounced because the next word starts with a vowel. Liaison helps connect the words smoothly.

Special Cases and Exceptions

As with many rules in language, there are exceptions. Some nouns that end in "-e" are actually masculine, like le problème (luh pro-blem) - the problem. Similarly, some nouns that don't end in "-e" are feminine, like la main (lah man) - the hand. It's important to learn these exceptions as you encounter them.

Another special case is when talking about groups of mixed gender. In French, if a group includes both males and females, you use the masculine plural form. For example:

Les étudiants (lay zay-tyoo-dyon) - The students (mixed group)

Des amis (day zah-mee) - Some friends (mixed group)

Even if there is only one male in a group of females, the masculine form is still used. This is just one of the quirks of the French language!

Using Articles with Adjectives

When you add an adjective to describe a noun, the article still needs to match the gender and number of the noun. For example:

Le grand livre (luh grahn leevr) - The big book (masculine, singular)

La petite table (lah puh-teet tah-bl) - The small table (feminine, singular)

Les grands livres (lay grahn leevr) - The big books (masculine, plural)

Des petites tables (day puh-teet tah-bl) - Some small tables (feminine, plural)

The article le, la, les, or des changes depending on the noun, even when there's an adjective involved. The adjective itself may also change to match the gender and number of the noun.

Key Points to Remember:

1. **Definite and Indefinite Articles:** French articles change based on the gender and number of the noun. Le (masculine), la (feminine), l' (before vowels), and les (plural) are definite articles, while un (masculine), une (feminine), and des (plural) are indefinite articles.

2. **Gender of Nouns:** Every French noun is either masculine or feminine, which determines the article used. While there are some patterns (e.g., nouns ending in "-e" are often feminine), there are exceptions, so it's important to memorize the gender with each noun.

3. **Elision and Liaison:** When a noun starts with a vowel or silent "h," le or la becomes l' (elision). Additionally, liaison connects words smoothly when an article's final consonant is pronounced before a vowel, as in les amis (lay zah-mee).

4. **Special Cases:** Some nouns that don't follow typical gender rules, like le problème (masculine) and la main (feminine), should be memorized. For mixed-gender groups, the masculine plural form is used.

5. **Articles with Adjectives:** The article must match the gender and number of the noun even when an adjective is added. For example, le grand livre (the big book) vs. les grands livres (the big books).

Chapter 13

Singular and Plural Nouns

In this chapter, we're going to learn about **Singular and Plural Nouns** in French. Understanding how to form and use singular and plural nouns is essential because it helps you talk about one thing or many things. By the end of this chapter, you'll be able to recognize singular and plural nouns, form the plural from the singular, and use them correctly in sentences. Let's get started!

What Are Singular and Plural Nouns?

In French, as in English, nouns can be singular or plural. A singular noun refers to one person, place, thing, or idea, while a plural noun refers to more than one. For example:

Un livre (uhn leevr) - A book (singular)

Des livres (day leevr) - Some books (plural)

In the first example, livre (book) is singular, meaning there is only one book. In the second example, livres is plural, meaning there are multiple books. Notice how the article changes from un to des when the noun becomes plural.

Forming the Plural of Nouns

In French, most singular nouns are made plural by adding an "-s" at the end. However, this "-s" is usually not pronounced, so the word sounds the same in both singular and plural forms. Here are some examples:

Un chat (uhn shah) - A cat (singular)

Des chats (day shah) - Some cats (plural)

Une pomme (oon pohm) - An apple (singular)

Des pommes (day pohm) - Some apples (plural)

Even though you add an "-s" to form the plural, the pronunciation of the word doesn't change. You can tell it's plural by the context and the article used with the noun.

Irregular Plural Forms

Just like in English, some nouns in French have irregular plural forms. These nouns don't follow the standard "-s" rule. Let's look at a few common examples:

Nouns Ending in "-eau" or "-eu"

Nouns that end in "-eau" or "-eu" usually form their plural by adding "-x" instead of "-s." For example:

Un bateau (uhn bah-toh) - A boat (singular)

Des bateaux (day bah-toh) - Some boats (plural)

Un jeu (uhn zhuh) - A game (singular)

Des jeux (day zhuh) - Some games (plural)

In these examples, the plural form is created by adding "-x" to the end of the word, but the pronunciation remains the same.

Nouns Ending in "-al"

Nouns that end in "-al" usually form their plural by changing "-al" to "-aux." For example:

Un animal (uhn ah-nee-mal) - An animal (singular)

Des animaux (day zah-nee-moh) - Some animals (plural)

Un journal (uhn zhoor-nahl) - A newspaper (singular)

Des journaux (day zhoor-noh) - Some newspapers (plural)

Here, the ending changes from "-al" to "-aux," and the pronunciation also changes slightly.

Nouns That Stay the Same in Singular and Plural

Some nouns in French don't change at all when they become plural. Their singular and plural forms are identical. For example:

Un autobus (uhn oh-toh-bus) - A bus (singular)

Des autobus (day oh-toh-bus) - Some buses (plural)

Un prix (uhn pree) - A prize (singular)

Des prix (day pree) - Some prizes (plural)

In these cases, the noun doesn't change, and you rely on the article and context to know whether it's singular or plural.

Articles with Singular and Plural Nouns

As you've seen, the article changes when a noun goes from singular to plural. Let's review the articles you use with singular and plural nouns:

Singular:

Un (uhn) - A (used with masculine singular nouns)

Une (oon) - An (used with feminine singular nouns)

Le (luh) - The (used with masculine singular nouns)

La (lah) - The (used with feminine singular nouns)

L' (l) - The (used before a singular noun that starts with a vowel or silent "h")

Plural:

Des (day) - Some (used with both masculine and feminine plural nouns)

Les (lay) - The (used with both masculine and feminine plural nouns)

For example:

Un garçon (uhn gar-sohn) - A boy (singular)

Des garçons (day gar-sohn) - Some boys (plural)

La fille (lah fee) - The girl (singular)

Les filles (lay fee) - The girls (plural)

It's important to use the correct article to match the number of the noun.

Making Adjectives Agree with Plural Nouns

In French, adjectives (words that describe nouns) must agree in gender and number with the noun they describe. This means that when a noun is plural, the adjective must also be in its plural form. Most of the time, you make an adjective plural by adding an "-s" at the end. However, just like with nouns, this "-s" is usually not pronounced. Let's look at some examples:

Un chat noir (uhn shah nwar) - A black cat (singular, masculine)

Des chats noirs (day shah nwar) - Some black cats (plural, masculine)

Une pomme rouge (oon pohm roozh) - A red apple (singular, feminine)

Des pommes rouges (day pohm roozh) - Some red apples (plural, feminine)

In both examples, the adjective noir (black) and rouge (red) adds an "-s" to agree with the plural noun. The pronunciation of the adjective doesn't change, but the spelling does.

Special Cases: Collective Nouns

Sometimes, a noun in French might look singular but actually refers to a group of things or people, making it collective. For example, la famille (lah fah-mee) means "the family" but refers to more than one person. Even though it's singular in form, it can represent a group.

When using collective nouns, the article and verb forms will agree with the singular form of the noun, but it's understood that the noun represents a group. For example:

La famille est grande. (lah fah-mee eh grahnd) - The family is big.

Here, la famille is singular, so the verb est (is) is also singular, even though "family" refers to more than one person.

Using Numbers with Plural Nouns

When you're counting things in French, the noun stays plural after the number (except when the number is one). For example:

Un livre (uhn leevr) - One book

Deux livres (duh leevr) - Two books

Trois pommes (trwah pohm) - Three apples

Quatre chats (ka-truh shah) - Four cats

In these examples, the noun is plural after the number, and the article des isn't used because the number itself shows that the noun is plural.

Key Points to Remember:

1. **Singular vs. Plural Nouns:** Singular nouns refer to one item, while plural nouns refer to more than one. Most plurals are formed by adding an "-s," though the pronunciation often stays the same.

2. **Irregular Plurals:** Some nouns have irregular plural forms, such as those ending in

"-eau" or "-eu" (e.g., bateau becomes bateaux), and those ending in "-al" (e.g., animal becomes animaux).

3. **Articles for Singular and Plural:** Articles change based on singular or plural forms—un/une for singular "a," des for plural "some," and le/la/l' for singular "the," les for plural "the."

4. **Adjective Agreement:** Adjectives must agree in gender and number with the nouns they describe, usually by adding an "-s" for plurals.

5. **Collective Nouns:** Some singular nouns, like la famille (family), refer to groups but still take singular verbs and articles.

Chapter 14

Subject Pronouns

In this chapter, we're going to learn about **Subject Pronouns** in French. Subject pronouns are essential because they tell us who is doing the action in a sentence. Just like in English, where we use pronouns like "I," "you," "he," and "she," French has its own set of subject pronouns. By the end of this chapter, you'll know how to use these pronouns correctly and understand their importance in forming sentences. Let's get started!

What Are Subject Pronouns?

Subject pronouns are words that replace the subject of a sentence, which is the person or thing doing the action. In English, we use pronouns like "I," "you," "he," "she," "we," and "they." French has similar pronouns, but with a few differences that are important to learn.

Here are the French subject pronouns:

Je (zhuh) - I

Tu (tew) - You (informal)

Il (eel) - He

Elle (el) - She

Nous (noo) - We

Vous (voo) - You (formal or plural)

Ils (eel) - They (masculine or mixed group)

Elles (el) - They (feminine group)

These pronouns are used to replace the name of a person or group of people in a sentence. Let's explore each one in more detail.

Je (zhuh) - I

The pronoun je means "I" in French and is used when you're talking about yourself. For example:

Je parle français. (zhuh parl frahn-say) - I speak French.

Je is always lowercase unless it's at the beginning of a sentence. It's a simple yet important pronoun because it's all about you!

Tu (tew) - You (informal)

The pronoun tu means "you" and is used when you're talking to one person who is a friend, family member, or someone your age. For example:

Tu aimes le chocolat. (tew em luh sho-koh-lah) - You like chocolate.

Tu is the informal way of saying "you," so it's best used in casual situations. If you're talking to someone you know well, tu is the pronoun to use.

Il (eel) - He

The pronoun il means "he" and is used when talking about a male person or sometimes a masculine noun. For example:

Il est mon ami. (eel eh mohn ah-mee) - He is my friend.

Il can also be used to refer to a masculine noun, even if it's not a person. For example:

Il est grand. (eel eh grahn) - It (the object) is big.

Elle (el) - She

The pronoun elle means "she" and is used when talking about a female person or a feminine noun. For example:

Elle est ma sœur. (el eh mah suhr) - She is my sister.

Just like il, elle can also refer to a feminine noun:

Elle est petite. (el eh puh-teet) - It (the object) is small.

Nous (noo) - We

The pronoun nous means "we" and is used when you're talking about yourself and at least one other person. For example:

Nous allons au parc. (noo ah-lon oh park) - We are going to the park.

Nous is a versatile pronoun because it can refer to any group that includes the speaker. It's used in both formal and informal situations.

Vous (voo) - You (formal or plural)

The pronoun vous can mean "you" when you're talking to one person in a formal setting, or it can mean "you" when talking to more than one person. For example:

Vous aimez le café. (voo zay-may luh kah-fay) - You like coffee (talking to one person formally or to a group).

When in doubt, vous is the safer choice because it's more polite. Use vous when speaking to teachers, strangers, or in any formal situation. It's also the pronoun you'll use when addressing a group of people.

Ils (eel) - They (masculine or mixed group)

The pronoun ils means "they" and is used when you're talking about a group of males or a mixed group of males and females. For example:

Ils jouent au football. (eel zhoo oh foot-bol) - They play soccer.

Even if there's only one male in the group, you still use ils. It's the default plural pronoun when there's at least one male involved.

Elles (el) - They (feminine group)

The pronoun elles also means "they," but it's used exclusively for a group of females. For example:

Elles chantent bien. (el shanht byan) - They sing well.

If the group is entirely female, elles is the correct pronoun to use. It helps to specify that the group is made up of only girls or women.

Using Subject Pronouns in Sentences

Now that you know the French subject pronouns, let's see how they work in sentences. The subject pronoun usually comes before the verb, just like in English. Here are some examples:

Je mange une pomme. (zhuh mahnzh oon pohm) - I am eating an apple.

Tu vas à l'école. (tew vah ah lay-kohl) - You are going to school.

Il joue avec son chien. (eel zhoo ah-vek sohn shyan) - He is playing with his dog.

Elle regarde la télévision. (el ruh-gard lah tay-lay-vee-zyon) - She is watching television.

Nous lisons un livre. (noo lee-zon uhn leevr) - We are reading a book.

Vous parlez français. (voo parl-ay frahn-say) - You speak French.

Ils dansent ensemble. (eel dahn-sahnt ahn-sombl) - They are dancing together.

Elles écoutent de la musique. (el zay-koot duh lah mew-zeek) - They are listening to music.

In each sentence, the subject pronoun is the person or group doing the action. It's important to choose the correct pronoun based on who or what you're talking about.

Elision with Subject Pronouns

In French, there's a special rule called **elision** that affects some subject pronouns. Elision occurs when je is followed by a verb that starts with a vowel or silent "h." In these cases, the "e" in je is dropped, and it's replaced by an apostrophe. For example:

J'aime (zhem) - I like (instead of Je aime)

J'habite (zhah-beet) - I live (instead of Je habite)

This elision makes the sentence easier to pronounce and helps the words flow together smoothly. It's a small but important detail to remember when using je with certain verbs.

Formal and Informal "You"

One of the unique aspects of French is that there are two ways to say "you": tu and vous. Here's a quick reminder of when to use each one:

- **Use** tu when talking to one person who is a friend, family member, or someone your age.
- **Use** vous when talking to one person you don't know well, someone in a position of authority, or when speaking to more than one person (regardless of familiarity).

For example:

Tu es mon ami. (tew eh mohn ah-mee) - You are my friend. (informal)

Vous êtes mon professeur. (voo zet mohn pro-fes-seur) - You are my teacher. (formal)

Understanding when to use tu versus vous is important for showing respect and politeness in French conversations.

Gender and Number Agreement

In French, it's also important to pay attention to gender and number when choosing a subject pronoun. For example:

- If you're talking about a group of boys, you would use ils.

- If you're talking about a group of girls, you would use elles.

- If you're talking about a mixed group of boys and girls, you still use ils.

For example:

Ils sont mes amis. (eel sohn may zah-mee) - They are my friends. (masculine or mixed group)

Elles sont mes amies. (el sohn may zah-mee) - They are my friends. (feminine group)

The pronoun changes depending on who you're talking about, so always consider the gender and number of the people or things involved.

Key Points to Remember:

1. **French Subject Pronouns:** The main subject pronouns in French are je (I), tu (you, informal), il/elle (he/she), nous (we), vous (you, formal/plural), ils/elles (they, masculine/feminine).

2. **Elision with Pronouns:** Je becomes j' before verbs starting with a vowel or silent "h" for smoother pronunciation (e.g., j'aime).

3. **Formal vs. Informal "You":** Use tu for informal situations and vous for formal situations or when addressing multiple people.

4. **Gender and Number Agreement:** Use ils for a group of males or mixed gender, and elles for a group of females.

5. **Pronoun Placement:** Subject pronouns generally come before the verb in a sentence.

Chapter 15

Possessive Adjectives

In this chapter, we're going to learn about **Possessive Adjectives** in French. Possessive adjectives are important because they help us show ownership or possession, just like "my," "your," "his," and "her" do in English. By the end of this chapter, you'll know how to use these adjectives correctly to talk about things that belong to you or others. Let's get started!

What Are Possessive Adjectives?

Possessive adjectives are words that tell us who something belongs to. In English, we use words like "my," "your," "his," "her," "our," and "their" to show possession. French has similar words, but they change depending on the gender and number of the noun they describe.

Here are the French possessive adjectives:

For "my":

- **Mon** (mohn) - Used with masculine singular nouns
- **Ma** (mah) - Used with feminine singular nouns
- **Mes** (may) - Used with plural nouns (both masculine and feminine)

For "your" (informal):

- **Ton** (tohn) - Used with masculine singular nouns
- **Ta** (tah) - Used with feminine singular nouns
- **Tes** (tay) - Used with plural nouns (both masculine and feminine)

For "his" or "her":

- **Son** (sohn) - Used with masculine singular nouns
- **Sa** (sah) - Used with feminine singular nouns

- **Ses** (say) - Used with plural nouns (both masculine and feminine)

For "our":

- **Notre** (noh-truh) - Used with singular nouns (both masculine and feminine)
- **Nos** (noh) - Used with plural nouns (both masculine and feminine)

For "your" (formal or plural):

- **Votre** (voh-truh) - Used with singular nouns (both masculine and feminine)
- **Vos** (voh) - Used with plural nouns (both masculine and feminine)

For "their":

- **Leur** (luhr) - Used with singular nouns (both masculine and feminine)
- **Leurs** (luhr) - Used with plural nouns (both masculine and feminine)

Notice how the possessive adjectives change depending on the gender and number of the noun they describe. Let's explore each one in more detail.

Using "My" in French: Mon, Ma, Mes

When you want to say "my" in French, you need to choose between mon, ma, and mes depending on the noun you're talking about.

Mon is used with masculine singular nouns:

Mon frère (mohn frehr) - My brother

Mon livre (mohn leevr) - My book

Ma is used with feminine singular nouns:

Ma sœur (mah suhr) - My sister

Ma maison (mah meh-zon) - My house

Mes is used with plural nouns, whether they are masculine or feminine:

Mes amis (may zah-mee) - My friends

Mes livres (may leevr) - My books

For example:

Mon chien est petit. (mohn shyan eh puh-tee) - My dog is small.

Ma chatte est petite. (mah shaht eh puh-teet) - My cat is small.

Mes chats sont petits. (may shah sohn puh-tee) - My cats are small.

Notice how the possessive adjective changes to match the gender and number of the noun.

Using "Your" in French: Ton, Ta, Tes

When talking to someone informally, you use ton, ta, or tes to say "your."

Ton is used with masculine singular nouns:

Ton père (tohn pehr) - Your father

Ton vélo (tohn vay-loh) - Your bike

Ta is used with feminine singular nouns:

Ta mère (tah mehr) - Your mother

Ta chaise (tah shez) - Your chair

Tes is used with plural nouns, whether they are masculine or feminine:

Tes amis (tay zah-mee) - Your friends

Tes chaussures (tay sho-sur) - Your shoes

For example:

Ton ami est drôle. (tohn ah-mee eh drohl) - Your friend is funny.

Ta sœur est gentille. (tah suhr eh zhahn-tee) - Your sister is kind.

Tes livres sont intéressants. (tay leevr sohn an-tay-reh-sahn) - Your books are interesting.

Again, the possessive adjective changes based on the noun's gender and number.

Using "His" or "Her" in French: Son, Sa, Ses

In French, the words for "his" and "her" are the same: son, sa, and ses. The choice between them depends on the gender and number of the noun, not the owner.

Son is used with masculine singular nouns:

Son chien (sohn shyan) - His/Her dog

Son livre (sohn leevr) - His/Her book

Sa is used with feminine singular nouns:

Sa maison (sah meh-zon) - His/Her house

Sa voiture (sah vwah-tyoor) - His/Her car

Ses is used with plural nouns, whether they are masculine or feminine:

Ses amis (say zah-mee) - His/Her friends

Ses chaussures (say sho-sur) - His/Her shoes

For example:

Son frère est intelligent. (sohn frehr eh an-tay-lee-zhahn) - His/Her brother is smart.

Sa sœur est jolie. (sah suhr eh zhoh-lee) - His/Her sister is pretty.

Ses parents sont gentils. (say pah-rohn sohn zhahn-tee) - His/Her parents are kind.

Remember, the possessive adjective matches the gender of the noun, not the gender of the person who owns it.

Using "Our" in French: Notre, Nos

When you want to say "our" in French, you use notre for singular nouns and nos for plural nouns.

Notre is used with singular nouns, both masculine and feminine:

Notre maison (noh-truh meh-zon) - Our house

Notre école (noh-truh ay-kohl) - Our school

Nos is used with plural nouns, both masculine and feminine:

Nos amis (noh zah-mee) - Our friends

Nos livres (noh leevr) - Our books

For example:

Notre chat est mignon. (noh-truh shah eh meen-yohn) - Our cat is cute.

Nos professeurs sont gentils. (noh pro-fes-seur sohn zhahn-tee) - Our teachers are kind.

Using "Your" (Formal or Plural) in French: Votre, Vos

When talking to someone formally or when talking to more than one person, you use votre for singular nouns and vos for plural nouns.

Votre is used with singular nouns, both masculine and feminine:

Votre voiture (voh-truh vwah-tyoor) - Your car

Votre chien (voh-truh shyan) - Your dog

Vos is used with plural nouns, both masculine and feminine:

Vos enfants (voh zahn-fahn) - Your children

Vos livres (voh leevr) - Your books

For example:

Votre maison est grande. (voh-truh meh-zon eh grahnd) - Your house is big.

Vos amis sont drôles. (voh zah-mee sohn drohl) - Your friends are funny.

Using votre and vos shows respect or indicates that you are addressing more than one person.

Using "Their" in French: Leur, Leurs

To say "their" in French, you use leur for singular nouns and leurs for plural nouns.

Leur is used with singular nouns, both masculine and feminine:

Leur maison (luhr meh-zon) - Their house

Leur chien (luhr shyan) - Their dog

Leurs is used with plural nouns, both masculine and feminine:

Leurs amis (luhr zah-mee) - Their friends

Leurs livres (luhr leevr) - Their books

For example:

Leur professeur est sévère. (luhr pro-fes-seur eh say-vehr) - Their teacher is strict.

Leurs enfants sont adorables. (luhr zahn-fahn sohn ah-doh-rab-l) - Their children are adorable.

Just like with other possessive adjectives, the form of leur and leurs depends on whether the noun is singular or plural.

Special Case: Mon, Ton, Son with Feminine Nouns Starting with a Vowel

In French, when a feminine singular noun starts with a vowel or a silent "h," the possessive adjectives ma, ta, and sa change to mon, ton, and son for easier pronunciation. For example:

Mon amie (mohn ah-mee) - My (female) friend (instead of ma amie)

Ton histoire (tohn ees-twar) - Your story (instead of ta histoire)

Son école (sohn ay-kohl) - His/Her school (instead of sa école)

This change helps the sentence flow more smoothly and prevents awkward pauses.

Key Points to Remember:

1. **Possessive Adjectives in French:** Possessive adjectives change depending on the gender and number of the noun. For example, "my" can be mon (masculine), ma (feminine), or mes (plural).

2. **Gender Agreement:** The choice of possessive adjective (e.g., son, sa, ses for "his" or "her") depends on the gender of the noun being possessed, not the owner.

3. **Plural Forms:** Use notre and nos for "our," votre and vos for "your" (formal/plural), and leur and leurs for "their," depending on whether the noun is singular or plural.

4. **Special Case with Vowels:** When a feminine singular noun starts with a vowel or silent "h," ma, ta, and sa change to mon, ton, and son for easier pronunciation.

5. **Usage Across Contexts:** Choose the appropriate possessive adjective based on both the relationship with the person you're speaking to (formal vs. informal) and the noun's characteristics.

Chapter 16

Question Words

In this chapter, we're going to learn about **Question Words** in French. Question words are important because they help us ask questions to get information. Just like in English, where we use words like "what," "where," "who," and "how," French has its own set of question words. By the end of this chapter, you'll know how to use these words to ask a variety of questions in French. Let's begin!

What Are Question Words?

Question words are words that are used to ask for specific information. In English, these words include "what," "where," "who," "when," "why," and "how." In French, there are similar words that serve the same purpose. Learning these words will help you ask all kinds of questions, whether you're trying to find out someone's name, where they're going, or what time it is.

Common Question Words in French

Here are the most common question words in French:

Que / Qu'est-ce que (kuh / kes-kuh) - What

Qui (kee) - Who

Où (oo) - Where

Quand (kahn) - When

Pourquoi (poor-kwah) - Why

Comment (koh-mahn) - How

Combien (kohm-byen) - How much / How many

Quel / Quelle (kel / kel) - Which / What (used with a noun)

Let's explore each of these question words in more detail, along with examples of how to use them in sentences.

Que / Qu'est-ce que (kuh / kes-kuh) - What

Que and qu'est-ce que are used to ask "what" in French. The choice between the two depends on the structure of the sentence.

Que is used in short, direct questions:

Que fais-tu? (kuh fay-tew) - What are you doing?

Que is usually used with inversion, where the subject and verb switch places, as seen in fais-tu.

Qu'est-ce que is more common in everyday conversation and is used to ask "what" in longer, more complex questions:

Qu'est-ce que tu fais? (kes-kuh tew fay) - What are you doing?

This form is easier to use and is similar to how we ask questions in English, so it's a good choice for beginners.

Qui (kee) - Who

Qui is the French word for "who." It's used to ask about a person or people. Here are some examples:

Qui est-ce? (kee es) - Who is it?

Qui parle? (kee parl) - Who is speaking?

Qui can be used on its own or at the beginning of a question to inquire about someone's identity or role.

Où (oo) - Where

Où is the French word for "where." It's used to ask about the location of something or someone. Here are some examples:

Où est la maison? (oo eh lah meh-zon) - Where is the house?

Où vas-tu? (oo vah-tew) - Where are you going?

Où is essential for asking about places and directions.

QUESTION WORDS

Quand (kahn) - When

Quand is the French word for "when." It's used to ask about time. Here are some examples:

Quand est la fête? (kahn eh lah fet) - When is the party?

Quand viens-tu? (kahn vyen-tew) - When are you coming?

Quand helps you ask questions about when events will happen or have happened.

Pourquoi (poor-kwah) - Why

Pourquoi is the French word for "why." It's used to ask for reasons or explanations. Here are some examples:

Pourquoi pleures-tu? (poor-kwah plur-tew) - Why are you crying?

Pourquoi étudies-tu le français? (poor-kwah ay-tew-dee-tew luh frahn-say) - Why are you studying French?

Pourquoi is essential for understanding motivations and reasons behind actions.

Comment (koh-mahn) - How

Comment is the French word for "how." It's used to ask about the manner or way something is done. Here are some examples:

Comment ça va? (koh-mahn sah vah) - How are you?

Comment fais-tu cela? (koh-mahn fay-tew suh-lah) - How do you do that?

Comment is versatile and can be used in many different types of questions.

Combien (kohm-byen) - How much / How many

Combien is used to ask about quantity or amount. It can mean both "how much" and "how many" depending on the context. Here are some examples:

Combien ça coûte? (kohm-byen sah koot) - How much does it cost?

Combien d'enfants as-tu? (kohm-byen don-fahn ah-tew) - How many children do you have?

Use combien whenever you need to know a number or quantity.

Quel / Quelle (kel / kel) - Which / What

Quel and quelle are used to ask "which" or "what" when you are referring to a specific noun. Quel is used with masculine nouns, and quelle is used with feminine nouns. Here are some examples:

Quel jour est-ce? (kel zhoor es) - What day is it?

Quelle couleur préfères-tu? (kel koo-luhr pray-fehr-tew) - Which color do you prefer?

Quel and quelle are important for asking specific questions about choices or preferences.

Forming Questions with Question Words

Now that you know the basic question words in French, let's look at how to form questions using these words. There are a few different ways to structure questions in French:

1. Question Word + Est-ce que + Subject + Verb

This is a common and straightforward way to ask questions in French. For example:

Où est-ce que tu habites? (oo es-kuh tew ah-beet) - Where do you live?

Pourquoi est-ce que tu pleures? (poor-kwah es-kuh tew plur) - Why are you crying?

2. Question Word + Inversion (Verb + Subject)

This is a more formal way to ask questions and is often used in written French. For example:

Où habites-tu? (oo ah-beet-tew) - Where do you live?

Pourquoi pleures-tu? (poor-kwah plur-tew) - Why are you crying?

In this structure, the verb comes before the subject pronoun.

3. Question Word + Subject + Verb

This is a more casual way to ask questions and is similar to how questions are structured in English. For example:

Tu habites où? (tew ah-beet oo) - Where do you live?

Tu pleures pourquoi? (tew plur poor-kwah) - Why are you crying?

In this structure, the subject comes before the verb, and the question word is placed at the end.

Special Cases: Qui and Où with Être

When using qui and où with the verb être (to be), the question structure is slightly different:

Qui est-ce qui...? (kee es kee) - Who is it that...?

This structure is used when qui is the subject of the verb. For example:

Qui est-ce qui parle? (kee es kee parl) - Who is speaking?

Où est...? (oo eh) - Where is...?

This structure is used to ask where someone or something is. For example:

Où est le livre? (oo eh luh leevr) - Where is the book?

Key Points to Remember:

1. **Common French Question Words:** Learn key question words such as Que (What), Qui (Who), Où (Where), Quand (When), Pourquoi (Why), and Comment (How) to ask for specific information.

2. **Using "Que" and "Qu'est-ce que":** Que is used in short, direct questions, while Qu'est-ce que is more common in conversation for longer questions.

3. **Forming Questions:** Questions can be structured in different ways: Question Word + Est-ce que + Subject + Verb (e.g., Où est-ce que tu habites?), inversion (e.g., Où habites-tu?), or casual placement (e.g., Tu habites où?).

4. **Gender and Number with "Quel" and "Quelle":** Use Quel for masculine nouns and Quelle for feminine nouns when asking "Which" or "What."

5. **Special Structures:** Use Qui est-ce qui for "Who is it that...?" and Où est...? for asking about the location of something or someone.

Chapter 17

Common Phrases and Expressions

In this chapter, we're going to learn about **Common Phrases and Expressions** in French. Knowing these phrases will help you navigate everyday conversations, whether you're greeting someone, asking for help, or just being polite. By the end of this chapter, you'll be familiar with a variety of useful expressions that you can use in different situations. Let's dive in!

Basic Greetings

Let's start with some of the most common phrases you'll use every day: greetings. These are the first words you say when you meet someone, so it's important to get them right!

Bonjour (bohn-zhoor) - Hello / Good morning

This is the standard way to greet someone during the day. It's polite and can be used with anyone, whether you know them well or not.

Bonsoir (bohn-swahr) - Good evening

You use bonsoir to greet someone in the evening. It's similar to saying "good evening" in English.

Salut (sah-lew) - Hi / Bye

Salut is a more casual greeting, used with friends or people your age. It can also be used to say "bye" when you're leaving.

Au revoir (oh ruh-vwahr) - Goodbye

This is the most common way to say "goodbye" in French. You can use it in both formal and informal situations.

À bientôt (ah byan-toh) - See you soon

You can say à bientôt when you expect to see someone again soon. It's a friendly way to say goodbye.

Polite Expressions

Politeness is very important in French culture, so it's essential to know how to use polite expressions correctly. Here are some that you'll use often:

S'il vous plaît (seel voo pleh) - Please (formal)

S'il te plaît (seel tuh pleh) - Please (informal)

These phrases mean "please" and are used when asking for something. Use s'il vous plaît in formal situations or when speaking to more than one person, and s'il te plaît when talking to a friend.

Merci (mehr-see) - Thank you

Merci is the standard way to say "thank you" in French. It's polite and can be used in any situation.

Merci beaucoup (mehr-see boh-koo) - Thank you very much

If you want to express extra gratitude, you can say merci beaucoup, which means "thank you very much."

De rien (duh ryan) - You're welcome

When someone thanks you, you can reply with de rien, which means "you're welcome."

Pardon (par-dohn) - Excuse me / Sorry

You can use pardon when you want to get someone's attention or when you bump into someone by accident. It's a way to say "excuse me" or "sorry."

Excusez-moi (ex-kew-zay mwah) - Excuse me (formal)

Excuse-moi (ex-kewz mwah) - Excuse me (informal)

These phrases are also used to say "excuse me," but they are a bit more formal than pardon. Use excusez-moi in formal situations and excuse-moi with friends.

Introducing Yourself

When you meet someone new, it's important to know how to introduce yourself in French. Here are some key phrases you'll need:

Je m'appelle... (zhuh mah-pel) - My name is...

This is how you say your name in French. For example, if your name is John, you would say, Je m'appelle John.

Enchanté(e) (ahn-shahn-tay) - Nice to meet you

When someone introduces themselves to you, you can reply with enchanté, which means "nice to meet you." If you're a girl, you add an extra "e" at the end, but the pronunciation stays the same.

D'où viens-tu? (doo vyen tew) - Where are you from? (informal)

D'où venez-vous? (doo vuh-nay voo) - Where are you from? (formal)

These phrases are used to ask someone where they're from. Use d'où viens-tu with friends or people your age, and d'où venez-vous in more formal situations.

Je viens de... (zhuh vyen duh) - I'm from...

This is how you tell someone where you're from. For example, if you're from New York, you would say, Je viens de New York.

Common Questions

Here are some common questions that you might ask or hear in everyday conversation:

Comment ça va? (koh-mahn sah vah) - How are you?

This is the most common way to ask someone how they're doing. It's similar to saying "how are you?" in English.

Ça va bien, merci. (sah vah byan, mehr-see) - I'm fine, thank you.

This is a typical response to comment ça va. It means "I'm fine, thank you."

Quel âge as-tu? (kel ahzh ah tew) - How old are you? (informal)

Quel âge avez-vous? (kel ahzh ah-vay voo) - How old are you? (formal)

These phrases are used to ask someone's age. Use quel âge as-tu when talking to friends or people your age, and quel âge avez-vous in formal situations.

J'ai douze ans. (zhay dooz ahn) - I am twelve years old.

This is how you tell someone your age. Simply replace "douze" with your own age.

Expressions for Daily Activities

Here are some phrases you might use to talk about your daily activities:

Je vais à l'école. (zhuh vay ah lay-kohl) - I'm going to school.

This phrase is useful for telling someone that you're going to school.

Je fais mes devoirs. (zhuh fay may duh-vwahr) - I'm doing my homework.

You can use this phrase to talk about doing your homework.

Je joue avec mes amis. (zhuh zhoo ah-vek may zah-mee) - I'm playing with my friends.

This is a great phrase to use when you're talking about playing with your friends.

J'aime lire. (zhem leer) - I like to read.

If you enjoy reading, you can use this phrase to let others know.

Je regarde la télévision. (zhuh ruh-gard lah tay-lay-vee-zyon) - I'm watching television.

This phrase is useful when you're talking about watching TV.

Expressions for Asking for Help

Sometimes you might need to ask for help or directions. Here are some phrases that can help you in those situations:

Pouvez-vous m'aider? (poo-vay voo may-day) - Can you help me? (formal)

Peux-tu m'aider? (puh tew may-day) - Can you help me? (informal)

These phrases are used to ask someone for help. Use pouvez-vous m'aider in formal situations and peux-tu m'aider with friends.

Où est...? (oo eh) - Where is...?

This phrase is used to ask where something is. For example, if you're looking for the bathroom, you could say, Où est la salle de bain? (oo eh lah sahl duh ban) - Where is the bathroom?

Je suis perdu(e). (zhuh swee pehr-dyoo) - I'm lost.

If you're lost, you can use this phrase to let someone know.

Expressions for Eating Out

When you're eating out at a restaurant, these phrases will come in handy:

Je voudrais... (zhuh voo-dray) - I would like...

Use this phrase when ordering food. For example, Je voudrais une pizza (zhuh voo-dray oon peet-zah) - I would like a pizza.

L'addition, s'il vous plaît. (lah-dee-syon, seel voo pleh) - The bill, please.

This is how you ask for the bill when you're ready to pay.

C'était délicieux. (say-teh day-lee-syuh) - It was delicious.

If you enjoyed your meal, you can use this phrase to compliment the food.

Expressions for Apologizing

If you need to apologize for something, these phrases will help:

Je suis désolé(e). (zhuh swee day-zoh-lay) - I'm sorry.

This is the standard way to say "I'm sorry" in French. If you're a girl, you add an extra "e" at the end, but the pronunciation stays the same.

C'est ma faute. (say mah foht) - It's my fault.

Use this phrase to take responsibility if something is your fault.

Pardonne-moi. (par-dohn mwah) - Forgive me. (informal)

If you want to ask someone to forgive you, you can say pardon or pardonne-moi if it's a more personal apology.

Common Idiomatic Expressions

Finally, here are a few common idiomatic expressions that you might hear or use:

Ça y est. (sah ee eh) - That's it. / It's done.

This phrase is used to express that something is finished or ready.

Il pleut des cordes. (eel pluh day kord) - It's raining cats and dogs.

This expression is used when it's raining heavily, similar to the English expression "It's raining cats and dogs."

Avoir le cafard. (ah-vwahr luh kah-far) - To feel blue.

This phrase literally means "to have the cockroach," but it's used to say that someone is feeling down or sad.

Key Points to Remember:

1. **Common Greetings:** Use Bonjour for hello, Bonsoir for good evening, and Salut for informal hi or bye.

2. **Politeness:** Remember to use Merci for thank you, S'il vous plaît for please, and Pardon or Excusez-moi to apologize or get attention.

3. **Introducing Yourself:** Say Je m'appelle followed by your name, and reply with Enchanté(e) when meeting someone.

4. **Asking Questions:** Use Comment ça va? to ask how someone is, and Où est...? to ask where something is.

5. **Daily Conversations:** For ordering food, say Je voudrais..., and use Je suis désolé(e) to apologize.

Chapter 18

Telling Time

In this chapter, we're going to learn about **Telling Time** in French. Knowing how to tell time is an important skill, and it will help you talk about your daily schedule, make plans with friends, and understand when events are happening. By the end of this chapter, you'll be able to tell time in French and use it in sentences. Let's start!

How to Ask the Time

When you want to ask someone what time it is in French, you can say:

Quelle heure est-il? (kel uhr eh-teel) - What time is it?

This is the most common way to ask the time. You can use it anytime you need to know the current time.

Telling Time: The Basics

When telling time in French, the structure is a bit different from English. You start with the phrase Il est (eel eh) which means "It is," followed by the hour and minutes. Let's look at how to say each hour:

1:00 - Une heure (ewn uhr) - One o'clock

2:00 - Deux heures (duh zuhr) - Two o'clock

3:00 - Trois heures (trwah zuhr) - Three o'clock

4:00 - Quatre heures (ka-truh zuhr) - Four o'clock

5:00 - Cinq heures (sank zuhr) - Five o'clock

6:00 - Six heures (sees zuhr) - Six o'clock

7:00 - Sept heures (set zuhr) - Seven o'clock

8:00 - Huit heures (weet zuhr) - Eight o'clock

9:00 - Neuf heures (nuhf zuhr) - Nine o'clock

10:00 - Dix heures (dees zuhr) - Ten o'clock

11:00 - Onze heures (ohnz zuhr) - Eleven o'clock

12:00 - Douze heures (dooz zuhr) - Twelve o'clock

In French, the hour is always followed by the word heures (which means "hours"), except for 1:00, where you use une heure instead of un heure because heure is feminine.

Adding Minutes

When you need to add minutes to the hour, you simply add the number of minutes after the word heures. Here's how you say the time with minutes:

1:05 - Une heure cinq (ewn uhr sank) - One oh five

2:10 - Deux heures dix (duh zuhr dees) - Two ten

3:15 - Trois heures quinze (trwah zuhr kanz) - Three fifteen

4:20 - Quatre heures vingt (ka-truh zuhr van) - Four twenty

5:25 - Cinq heures vingt-cinq (sank zuhr van-sank) - Five twenty-five

6:30 - Six heures trente (sees zuhr trahnt) - Six thirty

If the time is exactly on the hour, you just say the hour, like Il est deux heures for 2:00. But when you add minutes, the number of minutes follows heures.

Quarter Past, Half Past, and Quarter To

There are special ways to say "quarter past," "half past," and "quarter to" in French:

1:15 - Une heure et quart (ewn uhr ay kar) - A quarter past one

2:30 - Deux heures et demie (duh zuhr ay duh-mee) - Half past two

3:45 - Quatre heures moins le quart (ka-truh zuhr mwan luh kar) - A quarter to four

Here's how these work:

- **Quarter Past:** You use et quart to say "and a quarter."

- **Half Past:** You use et demie to say "and a half."

- **Quarter To:** You use moins le quart to say "minus the quarter," meaning it's 15 minutes before the next hour.

For example:

Il est huit heures et quart. (eel eh weet zuhr ay kar) - It is 8:15.

Il est dix heures et demie. (eel eh dees zuhr ay duh-mee) - It is 10:30.

Il est onze heures moins le quart. (eel eh ohnz zuhr mwan luh kar) - It is 10:45.

These phrases are very common and useful when telling time.

Using "AM" and "PM" in French

In French, there isn't a direct equivalent of "AM" and "PM." Instead, you clarify the time of day by adding phrases like du matin (in the morning), de l'après-midi (in the afternoon), or du soir (in the evening). Here's how you do it:

8:00 AM - Huit heures du matin (weet zuhr dew mah-tan) - Eight in the morning

3:00 PM - Trois heures de l'après-midi (trwah zuhr duh lah-pray-mee-dee) - Three in the afternoon

9:00 PM - Neuf heures du soir (nuhf zuhr dew swahr) - Nine in the evening

For example:

Il est dix heures du matin. (eel eh dees zuhr dew mah-tan) - It is 10:00 in the morning.

Il est quatre heures de l'après-midi. (eel eh ka-truh zuhr duh lah-pray-mee-dee) - It is 4:00 in the afternoon.

Il est sept heures du soir. (eel eh set zuhr dew swahr) - It is 7:00 in the evening.

These phrases help you specify whether you're talking about the morning, afternoon, or evening.

Military Time in French

In many French-speaking countries, people often use the 24-hour clock, also known as military time. Here's how it works:

1:00 PM - Treize heures (trez zuhr) - Thirteen hours

2:00 PM - Quatorze heures (ka-torz zuhr) - Fourteen hours

3:00 PM - Quinze heures (kanz zuhr) - Fifteen hours

4:00 PM - Seize heures (sez zuhr) - Sixteen hours

5:00 PM - Dix-sept heures (dees-set zuhr) - Seventeen hours

6:00 PM - Dix-huit heures (dees-weet zuhr) - Eighteen hours

7:00 PM - Dix-neuf heures (dees-nuhf zuhr) - Nineteen hours

8:00 PM - Vingt heures (van zuhr) - Twenty hours

9:00 PM - Vingt-et-une heures (van-tay-ewn zuhr) - Twenty-one hours

10:00 PM - Vingt-deux heures (van duh zuhr) - Twenty-two hours

11:00 PM - Vingt-trois heures (van-trwah zuhr) - Twenty-three hours

12:00 AM - Zéro heure (zay-roh zuhr) or **Minuit** (mee-nwee) - Midnight

In the 24-hour clock, you continue counting the hours after noon. For example, 2:00 PM becomes quatorze heures (14 hours), and 9:00 PM becomes vingt-et-une heures (21 hours). This system is especially common in schedules, such as for trains or flights.

For example:

Le film commence à vingt heures. (luh feelm koh-mahnce ah van zuhr) - The movie starts at 8:00 PM.

Le train part à quinze heures trente. (luh tran par ah kanz zuhr trahnt) - The train leaves at 3:30 PM.

Practice Making Sentences with Time

Now that you know how to tell time in French, let's practice making some sentences:

Je vais à l'école à huit heures. (zhuh vay ah lay-kohl ah weet zuhr) - I go to school at 8:00.

Nous mangeons à midi. (noo mahn-zhon ah mee-dee) - We eat at noon.

Il est cinq heures du matin. (eel eh sank zuhr dew mah-tan) - It's 5:00 in the morning.

Le concert commence à dix-neuf heures. (luh kon-sair koh-mahnce ah dees-nuhf zuhr) - The concert starts at 7:00 PM.

With these phrases, you can talk about when things happen during your day and understand others when they tell you the time.

Expressions Related to Time

Here are a few common expressions that involve time:

À quelle heure...? (ah kel uhr) - At what time...?

For example: À quelle heure commence le film? (ah kel uhr koh-mahnce luh feelm) - What time does the movie start?

Il est temps de... (eel eh ton duh) - It's time to...

For example: Il est temps de partir. (eel eh ton duh par-teer) - It's time to leave.

De bonne heure (duh bon uhr) - Early

For example: Je me lève de bonne heure. (zhuh muh lev duh bon uhr) - I wake up early.

En retard (on ruh-tar) - Late

For example: Il est en retard. (eel eh on ruh-tar) - He is late.

À l'heure (ah luhr) - On time

For example: Elle est toujours à l'heure. (el eh too-zhoor ah luhr) - She is always on time.

These expressions are useful for talking about being early, on time, or late.

Key Points to Remember:

1. **Asking and Telling Time:** To ask the time in French, say "Quelle heure est-il?" To tell time, use "Il est" followed by the hour and minutes, like "Il est deux heures" for 2:00.

2. **Adding Minutes:** Minutes are added after the hour, such as "Il est trois heures quinze" for 3:15. Special terms include "et quart" for quarter past, "et demie" for half past, and "moins le quart" for quarter to.

3. **AM and PM:** Use phrases like "du matin" (in the morning), "de l'après-midi" (in the afternoon), and "du soir" (in the evening) instead of AM and PM.

4. **24-Hour Clock:** French often uses the 24-hour clock for schedules, where 1:00 PM is "treize heures" and 9:00 PM is "vingt-et-une heures."

5. **Time-Related Expressions:** Useful expressions include "À quelle heure...?" (At what time...?), "Il est temps de..." (It's time to...), "de bonne heure" (early), "en retard" (late), and "à l'heure" (on time).

Chapter 19

Describing Weather

In this chapter, we're going to learn about **Describing Weather** in French. Talking about the weather is something we do almost every day, so it's a useful skill to have in any language. By the end of this chapter, you'll know how to describe different weather conditions in French and use them in sentences. Let's begin!

Basic Weather Vocabulary

First, let's learn some basic words and phrases related to weather. These words will help you describe what the weather is like on any given day.

Le temps (luh tahn) - The weather

This is the general word for "weather" in French. You might hear it in phrases like Quel temps fait-il? (kel tahn feh-teel) - What's the weather like?

Il fait (eel feh) - It is

This phrase is used to describe the weather. You'll often see it followed by an adjective or noun that describes the weather condition.

Here are some common weather conditions:

Beau (boh) - Nice / Beautiful

Mauvais (moh-veh) - Bad

Froid (frwah) - Cold

Chaud (shoh) - Hot / Warm

Frais (fre) - Cool

Nuageux (nwah-zhuh) - Cloudy

Pluvieux (plu-vyuh) - Rainy

Ensoleillé (ahn-soh-lay-yay) - Sunny

Neigeux (neh-zhuh) - Snowy

Venteux (von-tuh) - Windy

These words are essential for describing what the weather is like. Let's see how to use them in sentences.

Describing the Weather: Il fait...

In French, to describe the weather, you often start with the phrase Il fait (eel feh), which means "It is." Here's how you can use it:

Il fait beau. (eel feh boh) - It's nice / It's beautiful.

This phrase is used when the weather is pleasant, like on a sunny day with clear skies.

Il fait mauvais. (eel feh moh-veh) - It's bad.

Use this phrase when the weather is not so great, like on a rainy or stormy day.

Il fait froid. (eel feh frwah) - It's cold.

This is how you say it's cold outside. You can use it when the temperature is low, and you need a jacket.

Il fait chaud. (eel feh shoh) - It's hot / It's warm.

This phrase is for those hot summer days when the sun is shining, and it's warm outside.

Il fait frais. (eel feh freh) - It's cool.

You can use this when the weather is a bit chilly, but not too cold—perfect for a light sweater.

Talking About the Sun: Il y a du soleil

To talk about sunny weather, you can use the phrase Il y a du soleil (eel yah dew soh-lehy), which means "It's sunny." For example:

Il y a du soleil aujourd'hui. (eel yah dew soh-lehy oh-zhoor-dwee) - It's sunny today.

This is a great phrase to use when the sun is shining brightly in the sky.

Cloudy Weather: Il y a des nuages

If it's cloudy, you can say Il y a des nuages (eel yah day nwahzh), which means "It's cloudy." For example:

DESCRIBING WEATHER

Il y a des nuages dans le ciel. (eel yah day nwahzh dahn luh syel) - There are clouds in the sky.

This phrase is useful on days when the sun is hidden behind the clouds.

Rainy Days: Il pleut

When it's raining, the phrase to use is Il pleut (eel pleuh), which simply means "It's raining." For example:

Il pleut beaucoup aujourd'hui. (eel pleuh boh-koo oh-zhoor-dwee) - It's raining a lot today.

You can also describe light rain or heavy rain by adding more detail:

Il pleut légèrement. (eel pleuh lay-zhair-mahn) - It's raining lightly.

Il pleut des cordes. (eel pleuh day kord) - It's pouring rain. (literally, "It's raining ropes")

These phrases will help you talk about the rain, whether it's just a drizzle or a downpour.

Snowy Weather: Il neige

When it's snowing, you say Il neige (eel nehj), which means "It's snowing." For example:

Il neige en hiver. (eel nehj ahn ee-vair) - It snows in winter.

If you want to describe heavy snowfall, you can add more detail:

Il neige beaucoup. (eel nehj boh-koo) - It's snowing a lot.

These phrases will be handy when talking about winter weather.

Windy Weather: Il y a du vent

To describe a windy day, use the phrase Il y a du vent (eel yah dew von), which means "It's windy." For example:

Il y a du vent aujourd'hui. (eel yah dew von oh-zhoor-dwee) - It's windy today.

If it's very windy, you can say:

Il y a beaucoup de vent. (eel yah boh-koo duh von) - There's a lot of wind.

These phrases will help you talk about breezy days.

Talking About the Temperature

When you want to talk about how hot or cold it is, you can use the following phrases:

Il fait vingt degrés. (eel feh van duh-gray) - It's twenty degrees.

Il fait zéro degré. (eel feh zay-roh duh-gray) - It's zero degrees.

These phrases help you describe the temperature, whether it's warm, cold, or freezing outside.

Seasons and Weather

Different seasons bring different weather. Here's how you can talk about the weather during each season:

Le printemps (luh pran-tahn) - Spring

Au printemps, il fait doux. (oh pran-tahn eel feh doo) - In the spring, it's mild.

L'été (lay-tay) - Summer

En été, il fait chaud. (ahn lay-tay eel feh shoh) - In the summer, it's hot.

L'automne (loh-ton) - Fall

En automne, il fait frais. (ahn oh-ton eel feh freh) - In the fall, it's cool.

L'hiver (lee-vair) - Winter

En hiver, il fait froid. (ahn ee-vair eel feh frwah) - In the winter, it's cold.

These phrases will help you describe the weather during different times of the year.

Weather Expressions

There are also some common expressions related to weather in French. Here are a few:

Il fait un temps de chien. (eel feh uhn tahn duh shyan) - The weather is terrible. (literally, "It's a dog's weather")

Use this phrase when the weather is particularly bad, like during a storm.

Il fait un froid de canard. (eel feh uhn frwah duh kah-n ar) - It's freezing. (literally, "It's duck-cold")

This expression is used when it's extremely cold outside.

Il y a un orage. (eel yah uhn oh-rahzh) - There's a storm.

This phrase is used when there's thunder, lightning, and heavy rain.

These expressions add some flavor to your descriptions and help you sound more natural when talking about the weather.

Key Points to Remember:

1. **Basic Weather Vocabulary:** Learn essential French words like le temps (weather), il fait (it is), and common weather conditions such as beau (nice), froid (cold), and pluvieux (rainy).

2. **Describing the Weather:** Use the phrase Il fait followed by an adjective to describe the weather, such as Il fait chaud (It's hot) or Il fait frais (It's cool). For specific conditions, use phrases like Il y a du soleil (It's sunny) or Il pleut (It's raining).

3. **Weather Expressions:** Familiarize yourself with common expressions like Il fait un temps de chien (The weather is terrible) or Il fait un froid de canard (It's freezing), which are often used to describe extreme weather conditions.

4. **Seasons and Weather:** Learn how to describe weather during different seasons, such as En été, il fait chaud (In summer, it's hot) or En hiver, il fait froid (In winter, it's cold).

5. **Talking About the Temperature:** Use phrases like Il fait vingt degrés (It's twenty degrees) to discuss temperature, helping you communicate how hot or cold it is outside.

Chapter 20

Basic Verbs and Conjugation

In this chapter, we're going to learn about **Basic Verbs and Conjugation** in French. Verbs are action words—they tell us what someone is doing, like "to eat," "to play," or "to speak." Understanding how to use verbs and how to change them to match the subject (the person doing the action) is essential for forming sentences in French. By the end of this chapter, you'll know how to conjugate some basic verbs in the present tense and use them in sentences. Let's get started!

What Is Conjugation?

Conjugation is when we change the form of a verb to match the subject. In English, we do this too, like when we change "I eat" to "he eats" by adding an "s." French works similarly, but the endings change more depending on who is doing the action.

Let's start with one of the most common verbs in French: **être** (eh-tr), which means "to be."

Conjugating "Être" (To Be)

Here's how être is conjugated in the present tense:

Je suis (zhuh swee) - I am

Tu es (tew eh) - You are (informal)

Il/Elle est (eel/el eh) - He/She is

Nous sommes (noo sohm) - We are

Vous êtes (voo zet) - You are (formal or plural)

Ils/Elles sont (eel/el sohn) - They are

Here's how you can use être in sentences:

Je suis étudiant. (zhuh swee ay-tew-dyon) - I am a student.

Elle est gentille. (el eh zhahn-tee) - She is kind.

Nous sommes amis. (noo sohm zah-mee) - We are friends.

Conjugating "Avoir" (To Have)

Another important verb is **avoir** (ah-vwahr), which means "to have." Here's how it's conjugated:

J'ai (zhay) - I have

Tu as (tew ah) - You have (informal)

Il/Elle a (eel/el ah) - He/She has

Nous avons (noo zah-vohn) - We have

Vous avez (voo zah-vay) - You have (formal or plural)

Ils/Elles ont (eel/el zohn) - They have

Here's how you can use avoir in sentences:

J'ai un chien. (zhay uhn shyan) - I have a dog.

Tu as une sœur. (tew ah oon suhr) - You have a sister.

Ils ont des livres. (eel zohn day leevr) - They have books.

Conjugating Regular "-ER" Verbs

Most French verbs are regular verbs that follow a pattern when conjugated. The most common type of regular verbs ends in "-er," like **parler** (par-lay), which means "to speak." Here's how you conjugate regular "-er" verbs:

Step 1: Start with the infinitive (the basic form of the verb), like parler.

Step 2: Remove the "-er" ending to find the stem: parl-.

Step 3: Add the appropriate ending based on the subject:

- **Je parle** (zhuh parl) - I speak

- **Tu parles** (tew parl) - You speak (informal)

- **Il/Elle parle** (eel/el parl) - He/She speaks

- **Nous parlons** (noo parl-on) - We speak

- **Vous parlez** (voo parl-ay) - You speak (formal or plural)
- **Ils/Elles parlent** (eel/el parl) - They speak

Here's how you can use parler in sentences:

Je parle français. (zhuh parl frahn-say) - I speak French.

Nous parlons anglais. (noo parl-on ahn-glay) - We speak English.

Ils parlent espagnol. (eel parl es-pan-yol) - They speak Spanish.

Other Regular "-ER" Verbs

Here are a few other common "-er" verbs that follow the same pattern:

- **Regarder** (ruh-gar-day) - To watch / To look at
- **Aimer** (ay-may) - To like / To love
- **Jouer** (zhoo-ay) - To play
- **Manger** (mahn-zhay) - To eat
- **Chanter** (shahn-tay) - To sing

Let's look at some examples:

Je regarde la télévision. (zhuh ruh-gard lah tay-lay-vee-zyon) - I watch television.

Tu aimes les chats. (tew em lay shah) - You like cats.

Nous jouons au football. (noo zhoo-on oh foot-bol) - We play soccer.

Ils mangent une pizza. (eel mahnzh oon peet-zah) - They are eating a pizza.

Elle chante une chanson. (el shant oon shan-son) - She is singing a song.

Conjugating Regular "-IR" Verbs

Another group of regular verbs ends in "-ir," like **finir** (fee-neer), which means "to finish." Here's how to conjugate regular "-ir" verbs:

Step 1: Start with the infinitive, like finir.

Step 2: Remove the "-ir" ending to find the stem: fin-.

Step 3: Add the appropriate ending based on the subject:

- **Je finis** (zhuh fee-nee) - I finish
- **Tu finis** (tew fee-nee) - You finish (informal)
- **Il/Elle finit** (eel/el fee-nee) - He/She finishes
- **Nous finissons** (noo fee-nee-son) - We finish
- **Vous finissez** (voo fee-nee-say) - You finish (formal or plural)
- **Ils/Elles finissent** (eel/el fee-nees) - They finish

Here's how you can use finir in sentences:

Je finis mes devoirs. (zhuh fee-nee may duh-vwahr) - I finish my homework.

Nous finissons le projet. (noo fee-nee-son luh pro-zhay) - We are finishing the project.

Ils finissent le repas. (eel fee-nees luh ruh-pah) - They are finishing the meal.

Other Regular "-IR" Verbs

Here are a few other common "-ir" verbs that follow the same pattern:

- **Choisir** (shwah-zeer) - To choose
- **Remplir** (rahm-pleer) - To fill
- **Réussir** (ray-oo-seer) - To succeed
- **Grandir** (grahn-deer) - To grow
- **Obéir** (oh-bay-eer) - To obey

Let's look at some examples:

Je choisis un livre. (zhuh shwah-zee uhn leevr) - I choose a book.

Tu remplis la bouteille. (tew rahm-plee lah boo-tay) - You fill the bottle.

Elle réussit à l'examen. (el ray-oo-see ah lehg-zah-mahn) - She passes the exam.

Nous grandissons chaque année. (noo grahn-dee-son shak ah-nay) - We grow every year.

Ils obéissent aux règles. (eel oh-bay-eess oh reg-luh) - They obey the rules.

Conjugating Regular "-RE" Verbs

The third group of regular verbs ends in "-re," like **vendre** (von-druh), which means "to sell." Here's how to conjugate regular "-re" verbs:

Step 1: Start with the infinitive, like vendre.

Step 2: Remove the "-re" ending to find the stem: vend-.

Step 3: Add the appropriate ending based on the subject:

- **Je vends** (zhuh von) - I sell
- **Tu vends** (tew von) - You sell (informal)
- **Il/Elle vend** (eel/el von) - He/She sells
- **Nous vendons** (noo von-don) - We sell
- **Vous vendez** (voo von-day) - You sell (formal or plural)
- **Ils/Elles vendent** (eel/el von-d) - They sell

Here's how you can use vendre in sentences:

Je vends des légumes. (zhuh von day lay-gum) - I sell vegetables.

Nous vendons notre voiture. (noo von-don noh-truh vwah-tyoor) - We are selling our car.

Ils vendent des fruits. (eel von-d day frwee) - They are selling fruits.

Other Regular "-RE" Verbs

Here are a few other common "-re" verbs that follow the same pattern:

- **Attendre** (ah-ton-druh) - To wait
- **Entendre** (on-ton-druh) - To hear
- **Perdre** (pair-druh) - To lose
- **Répondre** (ray-pon-druh) - To answer
- **Descendre** (day-son-druh) - To go down

Let's look at some examples:

J'attends mon ami. (zhuh-tahn mon ah-mee) - I'm waiting for my friend.

Tu entends la musique. (tew on-ton lah mew-zeek) - You hear the music.

Elle perd ses clés. (el pair say klay) - She loses her keys.

Nous répondons aux questions. (noo ray-pon-don oh kes-tyon) - We answer the questions.

Ils descendent les escaliers. (eel day-sond layz es-kah-lyay) - They are going down the stairs.

Key Points to Remember:

1. **Understanding Conjugation:** Conjugation is the process of changing the form of a verb to match the subject. In French, verbs change endings based on who is performing the action, similar to English but with more variations.

2. **Conjugating "Être" (To Be) and "Avoir" (To Have):** These are two essential verbs in French. Être is used to say "I am" (e.g., Je suis étudiant - I am a student), and Avoir is used to say "I have" (e.g., J'ai un chien - I have a dog).

3. **Regular "-ER" Verbs:** Regular verbs ending in "-er" follow a predictable pattern. For example, parler (to speak) conjugates as je parle (I speak), tu parles (you speak), etc. This pattern applies to many common verbs like aimer (to love) and manger (to eat).

4. **Regular "-IR" Verbs:** Verbs ending in "-ir" also follow a regular pattern. For instance, finir (to finish) becomes je finis (I finish), tu finis (you finish), etc. This pattern is consistent across other "-ir" verbs like choisir (to choose) and réussir (to succeed).

5. **Regular "-RE" Verbs:** Regular "-re" verbs like vendre (to sell) have their own conjugation pattern. For example, je vends (I sell), tu vends (you sell), etc. Other verbs following this pattern include attendre (to wait) and répondre (to answer).

Chapter 21

Present Tense Verbs

In this chapter, we're going to learn about **Present Tense Verbs** in French. The present tense is used to talk about actions that are happening right now or that happen regularly. Understanding how to conjugate verbs in the present tense is essential for everyday conversation. By the end of this chapter, you'll be able to conjugate and use present tense verbs in sentences. Let's dive in!

What Is the Present Tense?

The present tense in French is similar to the present tense in English. It's used to describe actions that are happening now, habits, or facts. For example, in English, you might say, "I eat," "He runs," or "We study." In French, you would use the present tense in the same way.

Regular Verbs in the Present Tense

Most French verbs are regular, which means they follow a predictable pattern when conjugated. Regular verbs in French fall into three main categories based on their endings: "-er," "-ir," and "-re." Let's start with the most common group: "-er" verbs.

Conjugating "-ER" Verbs

To conjugate a regular "-er" verb in the present tense, follow these steps:

Step 1: Start with the infinitive form of the verb (the basic form). For example, parler (par-lay), which means "to speak."

Step 2: Remove the "-er" ending to find the stem: parl-.

Step 3: Add the appropriate ending based on the subject:

- **Je parle** (zhuh parl) - I speak

- **Tu parles** (tew parl) - You speak (informal)

- **Il/Elle parle** (eel/el parl) - He/She speaks

- **Nous parlons** (noo parl-on) - We speak
- **Vous parlez** (voo parl-ay) - You speak (formal or plural)
- **Ils/Elles parlent** (eel/el parl) - They speak

Here are some examples of "-er" verbs in sentences:

Je chante une chanson. (zhuh shant oon shan-son) - I sing a song.

Tu écoutes de la musique. (tew ay-koot duh lah mew-zeek) - You listen to music.

Nous aimons les animaux. (noo ay-mon lay zah-nee-moh) - We love animals.

Conjugating "-IR" Verbs

Now, let's look at "-ir" verbs. To conjugate a regular "-ir" verb, follow these steps:

Step 1: Start with the infinitive form of the verb, like finir (fee-neer), which means "to finish."

Step 2: Remove the "-ir" ending to find the stem: fin-.

Step 3: Add the appropriate ending based on the subject:

- **Je finis** (zhuh fee-nee) - I finish
- **Tu finis** (tew fee-nee) - You finish (informal)
- **Il/Elle finit** (eel/el fee-nee) - He/She finishes
- **Nous finissons** (noo fee-nee-son) - We finish
- **Vous finissez** (voo fee-nee-say) - You finish (formal or plural)
- **Ils/Elles finissent** (eel/el fee-nees) - They finish

Here are some examples of "-ir" verbs in sentences:

Je choisis un livre. (zhuh shwah-zee uhn leevr) - I choose a book.

Elle réussit à l'examen. (el ray-oo-see ah lehg-zah-mahn) - She passes the exam.

Nous grandissons chaque année. (noo grahn-dee-son shak ah-nay) - We grow every year.

Conjugating "-RE" Verbs

The third group of regular verbs ends in "-re." Here's how to conjugate a regular "-re" verb in the present tense:

Step 1: Start with the infinitive form of the verb, like vendre (von-druh), which means "to sell."

Step 2: Remove the "-re" ending to find the stem: vend-.

Step 3: Add the appropriate ending based on the subject:

- **Je vends** (zhuh von) - I sell
- **Tu vends** (tew von) - You sell (informal)
- **Il/Elle vend** (eel/el von) - He/She sells
- **Nous vendons** (noo von-don) - We sell
- **Vous vendez** (voo von-day) - You sell (formal or plural)
- **Ils/Elles vendent** (eel/el von-d) - They sell

Here are some examples of "-re" verbs in sentences:

Je rends visite à ma grand-mère. (zhuh ron viz-eet ah mah grahn-mair) - I visit my grandmother.

Nous répondons aux questions. (noo ray-pon-don oh kes-tyon) - We answer the questions.

Ils entendent la musique. (eel on-tond lah mew-zeek) - They hear the music.

Irregular Verbs in the Present Tense

Not all French verbs follow the regular patterns we've just learned. Some verbs are irregular, which means they have unique conjugations that don't follow the usual rules. Let's look at a few of the most common irregular verbs.

Être (To Be)

The verb être (eh-tr) is highly irregular. Here's how it's conjugated in the present tense:

- **Je suis** (zhuh swee) - I am
- **Tu es** (tew eh) - You are (informal)
- **Il/Elle est** (eel/el eh) - He/She is
- **Nous sommes** (noo sohm) - We are
- **Vous êtes** (voo zet) - You are (formal or plural)

- **Ils/Elles sont** (eel/el sohn) - They are

Here are some examples of être in sentences:

Je suis étudiant. (zhuh swee ay-tew-dyon) - I am a student.

Elle est gentille. (el eh zhahn-tee) - She is kind.

Nous sommes amis. (noo sohm zah-mee) - We are friends.

Avoir (To Have)

Another important irregular verb is avoir (ah-vwahr), which means "to have." Here's how it's conjugated in the present tense:

- **J'ai** (zhay) - I have
- **Tu as** (tew ah) - You have (informal)
- **Il/Elle a** (eel/el ah) - He/She has
- **Nous avons** (noo zah-vohn) - We have
- **Vous avez** (voo zah-vay) - You have (formal or plural)
- **Ils/Elles ont** (eel/el zohn) - They have

Here are some examples of avoir in sentences:

J'ai un chien. (zhay uhn shyan) - I have a dog.

Tu as une sœur. (tew ah oon suhr) - You have a sister.

Ils ont des livres. (eel zohn day leevr) - They have books.

Faire (To Do/To Make)

The verb faire (fehr) is another irregular verb, and it's used often in French. Here's how it's conjugated in the present tense:

- **Je fais** (zhuh feh) - I do / I make
- **Tu fais** (tew feh) - You do / You make (informal)
- **Il/Elle fait** (eel/el feh) - He/She does / He/She makes
- **Nous faisons** (noo feh-zon) - We do / We make

- **Vous faites** (voo fet) - You do / You make (formal or plural)
- **Ils/Elles font** (eel/el fon) - They do / They make

Here are some examples of faire in sentences:

Je fais mes devoirs. (zhuh feh may duh-vwahr) - I do my homework.

Tu fais du sport. (tew feh dew spor) - You play sports.

Nous faisons un gâteau. (noo feh-zon uhn gah-toh) - We are making a cake.

Aller (To Go)

Aller (ah-lay) is another important irregular verb that means "to go." Here's how it's conjugated in the present tense:

- **Je vais** (zhuh veh) - I go
- **Tu vas** (tew vah) - You go (informal)
- **Il/Elle va** (eel/el vah) - He/She goes
- **Nous allons** (noo zah-lon) - We go
- **Vous allez** (voo zah-lay) - You go (formal or plural)
- **Ils/Elles vont** (eel/el von) - They go

Here are some examples of aller in sentences:

Je vais à l'école. (zhuh veh ah lay-kohl) - I go to school.

Tu vas au parc. (tew vah oh park) - You go to the park.

Ils vont au cinéma. (eel von oh see-nay-mah) - They go to the movies.

Key Points to Remember:

1. **Present Tense Usage:** The present tense in French is used to describe actions happening now, habits, or facts. It's essential for everyday conversation.

2. **Conjugating Regular Verbs:** Regular French verbs fall into three main categories: "-er," "-ir," and "-re." Each group follows a specific pattern when conjugated. For example, parler (to speak) becomes je parle (I speak), finir (to finish) becomes je finis (I finish), and vendre (to sell) becomes je vends (I sell).

3. **Irregular Verbs:** Some French verbs don't follow the regular conjugation patterns. Key irregular verbs include être (to be), avoir (to have), faire (to do/make), and aller (to go). Each of these has a unique set of conjugations that need to be memorized.

4. **Examples of Irregular Verb Usage:** Understanding how to use irregular verbs is crucial. For example, Je suis étudiant (I am a student), J'ai un chien (I have a dog), Je fais mes devoirs (I do my homework), and Je vais à l'école (I go to school) are all common phrases in French.

5. **Mastering the Basics:** To communicate effectively in French, mastering both regular and irregular verb conjugations in the present tense is vital. This forms the foundation for building more complex sentences.

Chapter 22

Negation

In this chapter, we're going to learn about **Negation** in French. Negation is how we turn a positive statement into a negative one, like changing "I am" to "I am not" in English. In French, negation has a specific structure that you need to follow. By the end of this chapter, you'll know how to form negative sentences and use them in conversation. Let's get started!

Basic Negation: "Ne...pas"

The most common way to make a sentence negative in French is by using the structure ne...pas. This is similar to adding "not" in English. The word ne (nuh) comes before the verb, and pas (pah) comes after the verb.

Here's how it works:

Step 1: Start with a positive sentence. For example: Je parle français. (zhuh parl frahn-say) - I speak French.

Step 2: Add ne before the verb and pas after the verb.

Step 3: The sentence now becomes negative: Je ne parle pas français. (zhuh nuh parl pah frahn-say) - I do not speak French.

Let's look at a few more examples:

Positive: Il mange une pomme. (eel mahnzh oon pohm) - He is eating an apple.

Negative: Il ne mange pas une pomme. (eel nuh mahnzh pah oon pohm) - He is not eating an apple.

Positive: Nous regardons la télévision. (noo ruh-gar-don lah tay-lay-vee-zyon) - We are watching TV.

Negative: Nous ne regardons pas la télévision. (noo nuh ruh-gar-don pah lah tay-lay-vee-zyon) - We are not watching TV.

Positive: Elles jouent au football. (el zhoo oh foot-bol) - They (feminine) play soccer.

Negative: Elles ne jouent pas au football. (el nuh zhoo pah oh foot-bol) - They (feminine) do not play soccer.

Notice how the structure ne...pas surrounds the verb to make the sentence negative. This is the basic rule for negation in French.

Negation with a Vowel or Silent "H"

When the verb begins with a vowel or a silent "h," the word ne changes to n' to make the sentence easier to pronounce. For example:

Positive: Il aime les chiens. (eel em lay shyan) - He likes dogs.

Negative: Il n'aime pas les chiens. (eel nem pah lay shyan) - He does not like dogs.

Here, ne becomes n' because the verb aime starts with a vowel.

Let's look at another example:

Positive: Elle habite à Paris. (el ah-beet ah pah-ree) - She lives in Paris.

Negative: Elle n'habite pas à Paris. (el nah-beet pah ah pah-ree) - She does not live in Paris.

Again, ne changes to n' because the verb habite starts with a silent "h."

Using "Ne...jamais" (Never)

To say "never" in French, you use the structure ne...jamais (zhah-may) instead of ne...pas. The word jamais replaces pas in the sentence. For example:

Positive: Il mange des légumes. (eel mahnzh day lay-gum) - He eats vegetables.

Negative: Il ne mange jamais de légumes. (eel nuh mahnzh zhah-may duh lay-gum) - He never eats vegetables.

Positive: Nous allons au cinéma. (noo zah-lon oh see-nay-mah) - We are going to the movies.

Negative: Nous n'allons jamais au cinéma. (noo nah-lon zhah-may oh see-nay-mah) - We never go to the movies.

Here, the word jamais is used to indicate that the action never happens.

Using "Ne...rien" (Nothing)

To say "nothing" in French, you use the structure ne...rien (ryan) instead of ne...pas. The word rien replaces pas in the sentence. For example:

Positive: Je fais quelque chose. (zhuh feh kel-kuh shohz) - I am doing something.

Negative: Je ne fais rien. (zhuh nuh feh ryan) - I am doing nothing.

Positive: Ils disent quelque chose. (eel deez kel-kuh shohz) - They are saying something.

Negative: Ils ne disent rien. (eel nuh deez ryan) - They are saying nothing.

Here, the word rien is used to indicate that nothing is happening or being done.

Using "Ne...plus" (No Longer / Not Anymore)

To say "no longer" or "not anymore" in French, you use the structure ne...plus (ploo). For example:

Positive: Je mange de la viande. (zhuh mahnzh duh lah vyahnd) - I eat meat.

Negative: Je ne mange plus de viande. (zhuh nuh mahnzh ploo duh vyahnd) - I no longer eat meat.

Positive: Elle habite ici. (el ah-beet ee-see) - She lives here.

Negative: Elle n'habite plus ici. (el nah-beet ploo ee-see) - She no longer lives here.

In these sentences, plus is used to indicate that the action that used to happen does not happen anymore.

Using "Ne...personne" (No One / Nobody)

To say "no one" or "nobody" in French, you use the structure ne...personne (pair-son). For example:

Positive: Quelqu'un parle. (kel-kun parl) - Someone is speaking.

Negative: Personne ne parle. (pair-son nuh parl) - No one is speaking.

Positive: Ils voient quelqu'un. (eel vwah kel-kun) - They see someone.

Negative: Ils ne voient personne. (eel nuh vwah pair-son) - They see no one.

Here, the word personne is used to indicate that nobody is doing the action or that nobody is involved.

Using "Ne...ni...ni" (Neither...nor)

To say "neither...nor" in French, you use the structure ne...ni...ni (nee). For example:

Positive: Je veux du chocolat ou de la glace. (zhuh vuh dew shoh-koh-lah oo duh lah gl ahs) - I want chocolate or ice cream.

Negative: Je ne veux ni chocolat ni glace. (zhuh nuh vuh nee shoh-koh-lah nee glahs) - I want neither chocolate nor ice cream.

Positive: Ils aiment les chiens et les chats. (eel em lay shyan ay lay shah) - They like dogs and cats.

Negative: Ils n'aiment ni les chiens ni les chats. (eel nem nee lay shyan nee lay shah) - They like neither dogs nor cats.

This structure is used to express that you don't want or like either of the options presented.

Special Cases with Negation

When using negation with the verbs être (to be) or avoir (to have), the structure remains the same. However, if you're using a compound tense like the passé composé, ne and pas go around the auxiliary verb (the helping verb).

For example, in the passé composé:

Positive: J'ai mangé une pomme. (zhay mahn-zhay oon pohm) - I ate an apple.

Negative: Je n'ai pas mangé de pomme. (zhuh nay pah mahn-zhay duh pohm) - I did not eat an apple.

Here, ne and pas go around the auxiliary verb ai (have), not the main verb mangé (eaten).

Key Points to Remember:

1. **Basic Negation with "Ne...pas"**: In French, negation is formed using the structure "ne...pas," which surrounds the verb to create a negative sentence. For example, Je parle français (I speak French) becomes Je ne parle pas français (I do not speak French).

2. **Negation with Vowels or Silent "H"**: When the verb begins with a vowel or a silent "h," "ne" changes to "n'" for easier pronunciation. For example, Il aime les chiens (He likes dogs) becomes Il n'aime pas les chiens (He does not like dogs).

3. **Using "Ne...jamais" for "Never"**: Replace "pas" with "jamais" to say "never." For instance, Il ne mange jamais de légumes means "He never eats vegetables."

4. **Other Negation Forms**: Different negation forms include ne...rien (nothing), ne...plus (no longer), and ne...personne (no one). Each structure replaces "pas" to convey specific negative meanings.

5. **Special Cases and Compound Tenses**: In compound tenses like the passé composé, the "ne...pas" structure surrounds the auxiliary verb. For example, Je n'ai pas mangé de pomme (I did not eat an apple).

Chapter 23

Introduction to Adjectives

In this chapter, we're going to learn about **Adjectives** in French. Adjectives are words that describe nouns. They tell us more about a person, place, or thing, like whether something is big, small, happy, or sad. Understanding how to use adjectives correctly will help you add more detail to your sentences. By the end of this chapter, you'll know how to use adjectives in French and how they change based on gender and number. Let's get started!

What Are Adjectives?

Adjectives are words that describe or give more information about a noun. In English, adjectives usually come before the noun they describe. For example, "a red apple" or "a tall building." In French, adjectives can come before or after the noun, depending on the adjective.

Here are some examples of adjectives in English and their French equivalents:

Big - Grand(e) (grahn/grahn-d)

Small - Petit(e) (puh-tee/puh-teet)

Happy - Heureux/Heureuse (uh-ruh/uh-ruhz)

Sad - Triste (treest)

Beautiful - Beau/Belle (boh/bell)

Old - Vieux/Vieille (vyuh/vyay)

Notice that some adjectives have different forms for masculine and feminine. We'll talk more about this later.

Where Do Adjectives Go in a Sentence?

In French, most adjectives come after the noun they describe. This is different from English, where adjectives usually come before the noun. For example:

English: a small cat

French: un chat petit (uhn shah puh-tee)

However, some common adjectives, especially those that describe beauty, age, goodness, or size (often remembered with the acronym BAGS), come before the noun. For example:

English: a beautiful house

French: une belle maison (oon bell meh-zon)

Here are a few more examples:

Un grand arbre (uhn grahn arbr) - A tall tree

Une petite voiture (oon puh-teet vwah-tyoor) - A small car

Un vieux livre (uhn vyuh leevr) - An old book

Most adjectives, though, follow the noun:

Un chien noir (uhn shyan nwahr) - A black dog

Une fleur rouge (oon flur roozh) - A red flower

Adjective Agreement: Gender and Number

In French, adjectives must agree in gender (masculine or feminine) and number (singular or plural) with the noun they describe. This means that the form of the adjective can change depending on whether the noun is masculine or feminine, and whether it's singular or plural.

Let's start with gender:

Masculine and Feminine Adjectives

For many adjectives, the masculine form is the base form. To make the adjective feminine, you often add an "-e" at the end. For example:

Masculine: Petit (puh-tee) - Small

Feminine: Petite (puh-teet) - Small

Masculine: Heureux (uh-ruh) - Happy

Feminine: Heureuse (uh-ruhz) - Happy

Not all adjectives follow this pattern, but many do. Let's look at some examples in sentences:

Un petit garçon (uhn puh-tee gar-son) - A small boy

Une petite fille (oon puh-teet fee-yuh) - A small girl

Un chien heureux (uhn shyan uh-ruh) - A happy dog (male)

Une chatte heureuse (oon shaht uh-ruhz) - A happy cat (female)

In these examples, you can see how the adjective changes to match the gender of the noun.

Singular and Plural Adjectives

Adjectives also change based on whether the noun is singular or plural. To make an adjective plural, you usually add an "-s" at the end, just like you do with nouns. For example:

Singular: Petit (puh-tee) - Small

Plural: Petits (puh-tee) - Small (more than one)

Singular: Heureuse (uh-ruhz) - Happy

Plural: Heureuses (uh-ruhz) - Happy (more than one)

Let's look at some examples:

Un grand arbre (uhn grahn arbr) - A tall tree

Des grands arbres (day grahn zarbr) - Tall trees

Une belle fleur (oon bell flur) - A beautiful flower

Des belles fleurs (day bell flur) - Beautiful flowers

Even though the pronunciation often stays the same, the spelling of the adjective changes to show whether it's describing one thing or many.

Irregular Adjectives

While many adjectives follow the rules we've just discussed, some are irregular and have unique forms. For example:

Beau (Masculine Singular) (boh) - Beautiful

Belle (Feminine Singular) (bell) - Beautiful

Beaux (Masculine Plural) (boh) - Beautiful

Belles (Feminine Plural) (bell) - Beautiful

Another example is **vieux** (vyuh), which means "old":

Vieux (Masculine Singular/Plural) (vyuh) - Old

Vieille (Feminine Singular) (vyay) - Old

Vieilles (Feminine Plural) (vyay) - Old

Here are some examples in sentences:

Un vieux livre (uhn vyuh leevr) - An old book

Une vieille maison (oon vyay meh-zon) - An old house

Des beaux vêtements (day boh vet-mahn) - Beautiful clothes

Des vieilles chaussures (day vyay shoh-sur) - Old shoes

These irregular adjectives require a bit of extra memorization, but with practice, they'll become easier to use.

Common Adjectives You Should Know

Here are some common adjectives you'll find useful as you start learning French:

Bon/Bonne (bohn/bonn) - Good

Mauvais/Mauvaise (moh-veh/moh-vez) - Bad

Grand/Grande (grahn/grahn-d) - Big/Tall

Petit/Petite (puh-tee/puh-teet) - Small

Intelligent/Intelligente (an-tay-lee-zhon/an-tay-lee-zhont) - Smart

Amusant/Amusante (ah-mew-zon/ah-mew-zont) - Funny

Jeune (zhuhn) - Young

Vieux/Vieille (vyuh/vyay) - Old

These adjectives will help you describe people, places, and things in a variety of situations.

Using Adjectives in Sentences

Let's put it all together and see how you can use adjectives in sentences:

J'ai une grande maison. (zhay oon grahn meh-zon) - I have a big house.

Elle porte une robe rouge. (el port oon rob roozh) - She is wearing a red dress.

Nous avons un petit chien. (noo zah-von uhn puh-tee shyan) - We have a small dog.

Il est un homme intelligent. (eel eh uhn om an-tay-lee-zhon) - He is a smart man.

Remember to match the adjective with the gender and number of the noun it describes. This will make your French sentences more accurate and clear.

Key Points to Remember:

1. **Adjective Placement**: In French, adjectives typically come after the noun they describe, except for some common adjectives (like those related to beauty, age, goodness, and size) which come before the noun. For example, un chat petit (a small cat) and une belle maison (a beautiful house).

2. **Gender Agreement**: Adjectives must agree in gender with the noun they describe. Masculine adjectives often add an "e" to become feminine. For example, petit (small, masculine) becomes petite (small, feminine).

3. **Number Agreement**: Adjectives also change based on the number of nouns they describe. To make an adjective plural, add an "-s" at the end. For instance, petit (singular) becomes petits (plural) for multiple small items.

4. **Irregular Adjectives**: Some adjectives have irregular forms that don't follow standard rules, like beau (beautiful) and vieux (old), which have different forms depending on gender and number.

5. **Common Adjectives**: Familiarize yourself with commonly used adjectives like bon/bonne (good), mauvais/mauvaise (bad), and jeune (young) to enhance your descriptive abilities in French.

Chapter 24

Comparisons and Superlatives

In this chapter, we're going to learn about **Comparisons and Superlatives** in French. Comparisons help us talk about how two or more things are similar or different, while superlatives let us express the highest or lowest degree of something. By the end of this chapter, you'll be able to make comparisons and use superlatives in your French sentences. Let's get started!

Comparisons: More, Less, and As...As

To compare things in French, you'll use words like plus (more), moins (less), and aussi (as). Let's start by learning how to compare two things.

More...than: Plus...que

If you want to say that something has more of a quality than something else, you use plus...que (ploos kuh). For example:

Mon chien est plus grand que ton chat. (mohn shyan eh ploo grahn kuh ton shah) - My dog is bigger than your cat.

Here, plus means "more," and que means "than." Together, they form "more...than."

Let's look at another example:

Elle est plus intelligente que lui. (el eh ploo an-tay-lee-zhont kuh lwee) - She is more intelligent than him.

In this sentence, plus intelligente que means "more intelligent than."

Less...than: Moins...que

If you want to say that something has less of a quality than something else, you use moins...que (mwan kuh). For example:

Ce film est moins intéressant que le livre. (suh feem eh mwan an-tay-reh-sahn kuh luh leevr) - This movie is less interesting than the book.

Here, moins means "less," and que means "than." Together, they form "less...than."

Another example:

Il est moins rapide que sa sœur. (eel eh mwan rah-peed kuh sah suhr) - He is less fast than his sister.

In this sentence, moins rapide que means "less fast than."

As...as: Aussi...que

If you want to say that two things are equal in some way, you use aussi...que (oh-see kuh). For example:

Mon frère est aussi grand que moi. (mohn frehr eh oh-see grahn kuh mwah) - My brother is as tall as me.

Here, aussi means "as," and que means "as." Together, they form "as...as."

Let's look at another example:

Elle est aussi gentille que toi. (el eh oh-see zhahn-tee kuh twah) - She is as kind as you.

In this sentence, aussi gentille que means "as kind as."

Making Comparisons with Nouns

Sometimes you might want to compare the quantity of nouns, like "more apples" or "less homework." Here's how you can do that in French.

More...than: Plus de...que

If you want to say that someone has more of something than someone else, you use plus de...que. For example:

J'ai plus de pommes que toi. (zhay ploo duh pom kuh twah) - I have more apples than you.

Here, plus de means "more of," and que means "than."

Another example:

Elle a plus de devoirs que moi. (el ah ploo duh duh-vwahr kuh mwah) - She has more homework than me.

Less...than: Moins de...que

If you want to say that someone has less of something than someone else, you use moins de...que. For example:

J'ai moins de livres que lui. (zhay mwan duh leevr kuh lwee) - I have fewer books than him.

Here, moins de means "less of," and que means "than."

Another example:

Ils ont moins de temps que nous. (eelz ohn mwan duh tahn kuh noo) - They have less time than us.

As much/as many...as: Autant de...que

If you want to say that two people have the same amount of something, you use autant de...que (oh-tahn duh kuh). For example:

J'ai autant de jouets que toi. (zhay oh-tahn duh zhweh kuh twah) - I have as many toys as you.

Here, autant de means "as much/as many of," and que means "as."

Another example:

Elle a autant de travail que moi. (el ah oh-tahn duh tra-vahy kuh mwah) - She has as much work as me.

Now that you know how to make comparisons, let's move on to superlatives.

Superlatives: The Most and The Least

Superlatives are used to express the highest or lowest degree of a quality. In English, we often add "-est" to the end of an adjective, like "biggest" or "smartest," or use "most" or "least" before an adjective, like "most beautiful" or "least interesting." In French, we use le/la/les plus (the most) and le/la/les moins (the least).

The Most: Le/La/Les Plus

If you want to say that something has the most of a quality, you use le plus (luh ploo) for masculine singular nouns, la plus (lah ploo) for feminine singular nouns, and les plus (lay ploo) for plural nouns. For example:

Mon frère est le plus grand. (mohn frehr eh luh ploo grahn) - My brother is the tallest.

Here, le plus grand means "the tallest."

Another example:

C'est la plus belle fleur. (seh lah ploo bell flur) - It's the most beautiful flower.

In this sentence, la plus belle means "the most beautiful."

Ils sont les plus intelligents de la classe. (eel sohn lay ploo an-tay-lee-zhon duh lah klass) - They are the most intelligent in the class.

Here, les plus intelligents means "the most intelligent."

The Least: Le/La/Les Moins

If you want to say that something has the least of a quality, you use le moins (luh mwan) for masculine singular nouns, la moins (lah mwan) for feminine singular nouns, and les moins (lay mwan) for plural nouns. For example:

Il est le moins rapide. (eel eh luh mwan rah-peed) - He is the least fast.

Here, le moins rapide means "the least fast."

Another example:

C'est la moins intéressante histoire. (seh lah mwan an-tay-reh-sahnt ees-twahr) - It's the least interesting story.

In this sentence, la moins intéressante means "the least interesting."

Ce sont les moins chers. (suh sohn lay mwan shehr) - These are the least expensive.

Here, les moins chers means "the least expensive."

Irregular Superlatives

Just like with adjectives, there are some irregular forms when it comes to superlatives. One of the most common is with the adjective bon (good) and mauvais (bad).

For "the best," instead of saying le plus bon, you say le meilleur (luh may-yur) for masculine singular, la meilleure (lah may-yur) for feminine singular, and les meilleurs (lay may-yur) for plural. For example:

C'est le meilleur gâteau. (seh luh may-yur gah-toh) - It's the best cake.

Elle est la meilleure élève. (el eh lah may-yur ay-lev) - She is the best student.

For "the worst," instead of saying le plus mauvais, you say le pire (luh peer) for masculine singular, la pire (lah peer) for feminine singular, and les pires (lay peer) for plural. For example:

C'est le pire film. (seh luh peer feem) - It's the worst movie.

Ils sont les pires joueurs. (eel sohn lay peer zhoo-er) - They are the worst players.

These irregular forms are important to remember because they are commonly used in everyday conversation.

Using Comparisons and Superlatives in Sentences

Now that you know how to form comparisons and superlatives, let's practice using them in sentences:

Mon frère est plus grand que moi. (mohn frehr eh ploo grahn kuh mwah) - My brother is taller than me.

Ce livre est moins intéressant que l'autre. (suh leevr eh mwan an-tay-reh-sahn kuh lohtr) - This book is less interesting than the other.

Elle est aussi intelligente que son ami. (el eh oh-see an-tay-lee-zhont kuh son ah-mee) - She is as smart as her friend.

C'est la meilleure pizza. (seh lah may-yur peet-zah) - It's the best pizza.

Ils sont les moins rapides de l'équipe. (eel sohn lay mwan rah-peeds duh lay-keep) - They are the slowest on the team.

These sentences show how comparisons and superlatives can add detail and precision to your descriptions, helping you express exactly what you mean.

Key Points to Remember:

1. **Making Comparisons**: Use plus...que (more than), moins...que (less than), and aussi...que (as...as) to compare qualities between two things. For example, "Elle est plus intelligente que lui" (She is more intelligent than him).

2. **Comparing Quantities**: Use plus de...que (more of than), moins de...que (less of than), and autant de...que (as much/as many of as) to compare quantities. For example, "J'ai plus de pommes que toi" (I have more apples than you).

3. **Superlatives**: Use le/la/les plus (the most) and le/la/les moins (the least) to express the highest or lowest degree of a quality. For example, "Mon frère est le plus grand"

(My brother is the tallest).

4. **Irregular Superlatives**: Some superlatives have irregular forms, such as le meilleur (the best) instead of le plus bon, and le pire (the worst) instead of le plus mauvais. These forms are essential to remember for accurate expressions.

5. **Usage in Sentences**: Apply comparisons and superlatives to describe relationships between objects or people, like "Elle est aussi intelligente que son ami" (She is as smart as her friend) or "C'est la meilleure pizza" (It's the best pizza).

Chapter 25

Food and Drinks

In this chapter, we're going to learn about **Food and Drinks** in French. Knowing how to talk about food and drinks is important because it helps you express what you like, what you want to eat, and what you're hungry or thirsty for. By the end of this chapter, you'll be able to name different foods and drinks in French and use them in sentences. Let's begin!

Basic Vocabulary for Food

Let's start by learning some common words for different types of food in French. Here are some basics:

Fruits - Les fruits (lay frwee)

Apple - Une pomme (oon pohm)

Banana - Une banane (oon bah-nan)

Orange - Une orange (oon oh-rahnzh)

Strawberry - Une fraise (oon frehz)

Grapes - Du raisin (dew ray-zan)

Vegetables - Les légumes (lay lay-gum)

Carrot - Une carotte (oon ka-rot)

Tomato - Une tomate (oon toh-mat)

Potato - Une pomme de terre (oon pohm duh tehr)

Lettuce - Une laitue (oon lay-tew)

Peas - Des petits pois (day puh-tee pwah)

Meats - Les viandes (lay vyahnd)

Chicken - Du poulet (dew poo-lay)

Beef - Du bœuf (dew buhf)

Pork - Du porc (dew por)

Fish - Du poisson (dew pwah-son)

Sausage - Une saucisse (oon soh-sees)

Dairy - Les produits laitiers (lay pro-dwee lay-tyay)

Milk - Du lait (dew lay)

Cheese - Du fromage (dew froh-mahzh)

Butter - Du beurre (dew buhr)

Yogurt - Du yaourt (dew yah-oor)

Ice cream - De la glace (duh lah glahs)

These words will help you talk about some of the most common foods. Now let's move on to drinks.

Basic Vocabulary for Drinks

Just like with food, it's important to know how to talk about drinks in French. Here are some key words:

Water - De l'eau (duh loh)

Juice - Du jus (dew zhuw)

Orange juice - Du jus d'orange (dew zhuw doh-rahnzh)

Milk - Du lait (dew lay)

Tea - Du thé (dew tay)

Coffee - Du café (dew kah-fay)

Soda - Du soda (dew soh-dah)

Hot chocolate - Du chocolat chaud (dew shoh-koh-lah shoh)

These are the most common drinks you'll encounter. Now that you know some basic vocabulary, let's learn how to use these words in sentences.

Talking About What You Like

To talk about what you like to eat or drink in French, you can use the verb aimer (ay-may), which means "to like." Here's how you can use it:

J'aime les pommes. (zhem lay pohm) - I like apples.

Tu aimes le fromage. (tew em luh froh-mahzh) - You like cheese.

Il aime les légumes. (eel em lay lay-gum) - He likes vegetables.

Nous aimons le chocolat. (noo zay-mon luh shoh-koh-lah) - We like chocolate.

Vous aimez le lait. (voo zay-may luh lay) - You like milk.

Elles aiment les fraises. (el zem lay frehz) - They (feminine) like strawberries.

Notice how the verb aimer changes to match the subject (the person who likes something). This is called conjugation, and it's important to remember when speaking French.

Talking About What You Want

To talk about what you want to eat or drink, you can use the verb vouloir (voo-lwahr), which means "to want." Here's how you can use it:

Je veux une pomme. (zhuh vuh oon pohm) - I want an apple.

Tu veux du jus. (tew vuh dew zhuw) - You want juice.

Il veut du pain. (eel vuh dew pan) - He wants bread.

Nous voulons des fruits. (noo voo-lon day frwee) - We want fruit.

Vous voulez du café. (voo voo-lay dew kah-fay) - You want coffee.

Ils veulent de la glace. (eel vuhl duh lah glahs) - They (masculine) want ice cream.

Using vouloir helps you express your desires, whether you're ordering in a restaurant or just talking about what you feel like eating.

Talking About Meals

In French, there are specific words for different meals of the day. Here's what they are:

Breakfast - Le petit-déjeuner (luh puh-tee day-zhuh-nay)

Lunch - Le déjeuner (luh day-zhuh-nay)

Dinner - Le dîner (luh dee-nay)

Snack - Le goûter (luh goo-tay)

Here's how you might talk about these meals:

Je mange des céréales au petit-déjeuner. (zhuh mahnzh day say-ray-al oh puh-tee day-zhuh-nay) - I eat cereal for breakfast.

Nous déjeunons à midi. (noo day-zhuh-non ah mee-dee) - We have lunch at noon.

Elle dîne avec sa famille. (el deen ah-vek sah fah-mee) - She eats dinner with her family.

Tu prends un goûter l'après-midi. (tew prahn uhn goo-tay lah-pray mee-dee) - You have a snack in the afternoon.

These phrases will help you talk about your daily meals in French.

Ordering Food and Drinks

If you're in a restaurant or café and want to order something, here's how you can do it in French. You can use the phrase Je voudrais (zhuh voo-dray), which means "I would like." For example:

Je voudrais une pizza. (zhuh voo-dray oon peet-zah) - I would like a pizza.

Je voudrais du jus d'orange. (zhuh voo-dray dew zhuw doh-rahnzh) - I would like orange juice.

Je voudrais un sandwich. (zhuh voo-dray uhn sahn-dweech) - I would like a sandwich.

Je voudrais une glace au chocolat. (zhuh voo-dray oon glahs oh shoh-koh-lah) - I would like chocolate ice cream.

This phrase is very useful when you're at a restaurant or café and want to order something to eat or drink.

Asking About Food Preferences

If you want to ask someone else about their food preferences, you can use the phrase Qu'est-ce que tu aimes...? (kes-kuh tew em), which means "What do you like...?" For example:

Qu'est-ce que tu aimes manger? (kes-kuh tew em mahn-zhay) - What do you like to eat?

Qu'est-ce que tu aimes boire? (kes-kuh tew em bwahr) - What do you like to drink?

These questions are great for starting a conversation about food and drinks in French.

Talking About Food You Don't Like

To talk about food or drinks you don't like, you can use the phrase Je n'aime pas (zhuh nem pah), which means "I don't like." For example:

Je n'aime pas les épinards. (zhuh nem pah lay zay-pee-nar) - I don't like spinach.

Je n'aime pas le café. (zhuh nem pah luh kah-fay) - I don't like coffee.

Using Je n'aime pas allows you to express your dislikes when it comes to food and drinks.

Common French Foods and Drinks

France is famous for its delicious food and drinks. Here are some popular French dishes and beverages that you might want to know about:

Baguette - Une baguette (oon bah-get) - A long, thin loaf of French bread.

Croissant - Un croissant (uhn krwah-sahn) - A buttery, flaky pastry.

Crêpe - Une crêpe (oon krep) - A thin pancake, often filled with sweet or savory ingredients.

Quiche - Une quiche (oon keesh) - A savory pie made with eggs, cheese, and sometimes vegetables or meat.

Escargot - Des escargots (dayz es-kar-goh) - Snails, often cooked in garlic butter.

Crème brûlée - Une crème brûlée (oon krem brew-lay) - A creamy dessert with a caramelized sugar topping.

Champagne - Du champagne (dew shahm-pahn-yuh) - A sparkling wine from the Champagne region of France.

These foods and drinks are not only delicious but also a big part of French culture.

Key Points to Remember:

1. **Basic Food Vocabulary**: Learn essential French words for common foods like les fruits (fruits), les légumes (vegetables), les viandes (meats), and les produits laitiers (dairy products). This will help you talk about a wide range of food items.

2. **Basic Drink Vocabulary**: Know key words for drinks such as de l'eau (water), du jus (juice), du café (coffee), and du thé (tea). This vocabulary is essential for discussing beverages in French.

3. **Talking About Preferences**: Use the verbs aimer (to like) and vouloir (to want) to

express what you like or want to eat or drink. For example, "J'aime les pommes" (I like apples) and "Je veux du jus" (I want juice).

4. **Ordering Food and Drinks**: When ordering in a restaurant or café, use the phrase Je voudrais (I would like) to politely ask for what you want. For instance, "Je voudrais une pizza" (I would like a pizza).

5. **Common French Foods**: Familiarize yourself with popular French dishes and drinks like une baguette (a baguette), un croissant (a croissant), une crêpe (a crepe), and du champagne (champagne). These are key parts of French cuisine and culture.

Chapter 26

Shopping and Currency

In this chapter, we're going to learn about **Shopping and Currency** in French. Whether you're buying clothes, food, or souvenirs, knowing how to talk about shopping and money in French is very useful. By the end of this chapter, you'll be able to ask for prices, talk about what you want to buy, and use basic French currency terms. Let's get started!

Basic Vocabulary for Shopping

First, let's learn some common words and phrases related to shopping. Here are some basics you'll need to know:

Store/Shop - Un magasin (uhn mah-gah-zan)

Shopping - Le shopping (luh shoh-peeng) or Les courses (lay koors) when referring to grocery shopping

Clothes - Les vêtements (lay vet-mahn)

Shoes - Les chaussures (lay shoh-sur)

Food - La nourriture (lah noo-ree-toor)

Money - L'argent (lar-zhahn)

Price - Le prix (luh pree)

Expensive - Cher (shehr) / Chère (shehr) (feminine)

Cheap - Bon marché (bon mar-shay)

These words will help you start your shopping adventure in French. Now let's learn how to ask about prices.

Asking About Prices

When you're shopping, one of the most important things to know is how to ask, "How much does this cost?" In French, you can say:

Combien ça coûte? (kohm-byen sah koot) - How much does this cost?

You can also ask about the price of a specific item by saying:

Quel est le prix de…? (kel eh luh pree duh) - What is the price of…?

For example:

Quel est le prix de cette chemise? (kel eh luh pree duh set shuh-meez) - What is the price of this shirt?

Combien coûtent ces chaussures? (kohm-byen koot say shoh-sur) - How much do these shoes cost?

These questions will help you find out how much something costs before deciding to buy it.

Talking About What You Want to Buy

When you're shopping, you might want to tell the salesperson what you're looking for. Here's how you can do that in French:

Je voudrais acheter… (zhuh voo-dray ash-tay) - I would like to buy…

For example:

Je voudrais acheter une robe. (zhuh voo-dray ash-tay oon rob) - I would like to buy a dress.

Je voudrais acheter des fruits. (zhuh voo-dray ash-tay day frwee) - I would like to buy some fruit.

You can also say what you're looking for with:

Je cherche… (zhuh sher-sh) - I'm looking for…

For example:

Je cherche un cadeau pour mon ami. (zhuh sher-sh uhn kah-doh poor mohn ah-mee) - I'm looking for a gift for my friend.

Je cherche des baskets. (zhuh sher-sh day bas-ket) - I'm looking for sneakers.

These phrases will help you communicate your needs while shopping in French-speaking areas.

Understanding and Using Currency: The Euro

In France and many other European countries, the currency used is the Euro. Here are some basic terms you need to know:

Euro - Un euro (uhn uh-roh)

Cents - Des centimes (day sahn-teem)

The symbol for the Euro is €, and it's usually written before the amount, like €5.00. For example:

Ça coûte cinq euros. (sah koot sank uh-roh) - It costs five euros.

Ça coûte deux euros cinquante. (sah koot duh uh-roh san-kahnt) - It costs two euros fifty.

If you want to ask if the price is in euros, you can say:

C'est en euros? (seh tahn uh-roh) - Is it in euros?

This is especially useful when traveling in Europe, where different countries might use different currencies.

Paying for Your Items

Once you've found what you want to buy, it's time to pay. Here's how you can handle the transaction in French:

Cash - En espèces (ahn es-pess)

Credit Card - Une carte de crédit (oon kart duh cray-dee)

Receipt - Un reçu (uhn ruh-sue)

If you want to pay with cash, you can say:

Je paie en espèces. (zhuh pay ahn es-pess) - I'm paying in cash.

If you want to pay with a credit card, you can say:

Je paie par carte. (zhuh pay par kart) - I'm paying by card.

After paying, you might want to ask for a receipt. Here's how:

Puis-je avoir un reçu? (pwee zhah-vwahr uhn ruh-sue) - Can I have a receipt?

These phrases will help you complete your purchase smoothly.

Asking for Help in a Store

Sometimes, you might need help finding something or understanding a price. Here are some useful phrases for asking for help in a store:

Pouvez-vous m'aider? (poo-vay voo may-day) - Can you help me?

Où est…? (oo eh) - Where is…?

For example:

Où est la caisse? (oo eh lah kess) - Where is the checkout?

Où sont les cabines d'essayage? (oo sohn lay kah-been dess-ay-ahzh) - Where are the fitting rooms?

These questions can help you navigate a store more easily.

Making a Decision

If you're not sure whether you want to buy something, you can use these phrases to help you decide:

C'est trop cher. (seh troh shehr) - It's too expensive.

Je vais réfléchir. (zhuh vay ray-flay-sheer) - I'll think about it.

Je vais le prendre. (zhuh vay luh prahndr) - I'll take it.

These phrases will help you communicate your decision to the salesperson.

Bargaining and Discounts

In some markets or smaller shops, it might be possible to negotiate the price. Here's how you can do that in French:

Est-ce que vous pouvez baisser le prix? (ess kuh voo poo-vay beh-say luh pree) - Can you lower the price?

C'est le meilleur prix? (seh luh may-yeur pree) - Is that the best price?

If there's a sale or discount, you might see the following terms:

Sale - Une vente (oon vahnt)

Discount - Une réduction (oon ray-dook-syon)

On sale - En solde (ahn sold)

For example:

C'est en solde? (seh ahn sold) - Is it on sale?

Quelle est la réduction? (kel eh lah ray-dook-syon) - What is the discount?

These phrases can help you save some money when shopping in French-speaking countries.

Common Shopping Scenarios

Here are some common scenarios you might encounter while shopping:

Vous avez cette chemise en taille M? (voo ah-vay set shuh-meez ahn tay M) - Do you have this shirt in size M?

Je voudrais essayer cette robe. (zhuh voo-dray ess-ay-yay set rob) - I would like to try on this dress.

Je ne trouve pas ce que je cherche. (zhuh nuh troov pah suh kuh zhuh sher-sh) - I can't find what I'm looking for.

Acceptez-vous les cartes de crédit? (ahk-sep-tay voo lay kart duh cray-dee) - Do you accept credit cards?

These sentences will help you navigate different shopping situations with ease.

Key Points to Remember:

1. **Basic Shopping Vocabulary**: Learn essential French words like magasin (store), vêtements (clothes), prix (price), and cher/chère (expensive). These terms are crucial for navigating shopping scenarios.

2. **Asking About Prices**: Use phrases like Combien ça coûte? (How much does this cost?) and Quel est le prix de...? (What is the price of...?) to inquire about the cost of items before purchasing.

3. **Talking About What You Want to Buy**: Express your shopping intentions with Je voudrais acheter... (I would like to buy...) or Je cherche... (I'm looking for...), making it easier to communicate your needs in stores.

4. **Understanding and Using Currency**: Familiarize yourself with the Euro currency, using terms like un euro (one euro) and des centimes (cents). Ask if prices are in euros with C'est en euros? (Is it in euros?).

5. **Paying and Asking for Help**: Know how to say Je paie en espèces (I'm paying in cash) or Je paie par carte (I'm paying by card). For assistance, ask Pouvez-vous m'aider? (Can you help me?) to navigate shopping more effectively.

Chapter 27

Directions and Locations

In this chapter, we're going to learn about **Directions and Locations** in French. Knowing how to ask for and give directions is an important skill, especially when you're in a new place. By the end of this chapter, you'll be able to ask for directions, understand basic location words, and give directions in French. Let's get started!

Basic Vocabulary for Directions

First, let's learn some basic words related to directions and locations. Here are some key terms:

Left - Gauche (gohsh)

Right - Droit (drwah)

Straight - Tout droit (too drwah)

Here - Ici (ee-see)

There - Là (lah)

Near - Près de (preh duh)

Far - Loin de (lwan duh)

In front of - Devant (duh-vahn)

Behind - Derrière (deh-ree-ehr)

Next to - À côté de (ah koh-tay duh)

Between - Entre (ahn-truh)

On the corner of - Au coin de (oh kwahn duh)

These words will help you talk about where things are and how to get to them. Now, let's learn how to ask for directions.

Asking for Directions

If you're lost or need help finding something, here's how you can ask for directions in French:

Où est...? (oo eh) - Where is...?

You can use this phrase to ask for the location of a specific place. For example:

Où est la banque? (oo eh lah bahnk) - Where is the bank?

Où est la station de métro? (oo eh lah stah-syon duh meh-troh) - Where is the metro station?

Où est le supermarché? (oo eh luh soo-pehr-mar-shay) - Where is the supermarket?

If you want to ask about more than one place, you can say:

Où sont...? (oo sohn) - Where are...?

For example:

Où sont les toilettes? (oo sohn lay twah-let) - Where are the restrooms?

Où sont les magasins? (oo sohn lay mah-gah-zan) - Where are the shops?

These questions are essential when you're navigating a new area and need to find specific places.

Understanding Directions

When someone gives you directions in French, they might use some of the following phrases. Let's break them down:

Allez tout droit. (ah-lay too drwah) - Go straight.

Tournez à gauche. (toor-nay ah gohsh) - Turn left.

Tournez à droite. (toor-nay ah drwah) - Turn right.

Continuez jusqu'au bout. (kon-tee-nway zhuhs-koh boo) - Continue to the end.

Traversez la rue. (trah-ver-say lah rew) - Cross the street.

If someone gives you directions, they might also include information about landmarks or buildings to help you find your way. For example:

La banque est à côté de la poste. (lah bahnk eh ah koh-tay duh lah post) - The bank is next to the post office.

Le musée est en face de l'hôtel. (luh mew-zay eh ahn fahss duh loh-tel) - The museum is across from the hotel.

Le parc est derrière l'église. (luh park eh deh-ree-ehr lay-gleez) - The park is behind the church.

Understanding these phrases will help you follow directions more easily.

Giving Directions

Now that you know how to ask for directions and understand them, let's learn how to give directions. This is useful if someone asks you for help, or if you want to explain how to get somewhere. Here are some common phrases you can use:

Allez tout droit, puis tournez à gauche. (ah-lay too drwah pwee toor-nay ah gohsh) - Go straight, then turn left.

Tournez à droite après le feu. (toor-nay ah drwah ah-pray luh fuh) - Turn right after the traffic light.

La pharmacie est à gauche, en face du café. (lah far-mah-see eh ah gohsh ahn fahss dew kah-fay) - The pharmacy is on the left, across from the café.

Continuez jusqu'au bout de la rue. (kon-tee-nway zhuhs-koh boo duh lah rew) - Continue to the end of the street.

These sentences will help you guide someone to their destination or explain how to get somewhere.

Describing Locations

To talk about where things are located, you can use some of the location words we learned earlier. Here are some examples:

Le parc est près de l'école. (luh park eh preh duh lay-kohl) - The park is near the school.

Le cinéma est loin de ma maison. (luh see-nay-mah eh lwan duh mah may-zon) - The cinema is far from my house.

La bibliothèque est à côté du musée. (lah bee-blee-oh-tek eh ah koh-tay dew mew-zay) - The library is next to the museum.

Le restaurant est au coin de la rue. (luh res-toh-rahn eh oh kwahn duh lah rew) - The restaurant is on the corner of the street.

These examples show you how to describe where things are in relation to each other.

Asking for Specific Locations

If you're looking for a specific type of place, here's how you can ask for it in French:

Où est le restaurant le plus proche? (oo eh luh res-toh-rahn luh ploo prohsh) - Where is the nearest restaurant?

Où est la pharmacie la plus proche? (oo eh lah far-mah-see lah ploo prohsh) - Where is the nearest pharmacy?

Où est la station de métro la plus proche? (oo eh lah stah-syon duh meh-troh lah ploo prohsh) - Where is the nearest metro station?

You can use the phrase le plus proche (luh ploo prohsh) to ask for the nearest location of something.

Describing How to Get Somewhere

Sometimes, you might need to describe how to get somewhere in more detail. Here are some phrases that can help:

Pour aller à la gare, prenez cette rue et continuez tout droit. (poor ah-lay ah lah gar pruh-nay set rew eh kon-tee-nway too drwah) - To get to the train station, take this street and go straight.

Marchez jusqu'au carrefour, puis tournez à droite. (mar-shay zhuhs-koh kar-foohr pwee toor-nay ah drwah) - Walk to the intersection, then turn right.

Le musée est au bout de cette rue, à gauche. (luh mew-zay eh oh boo duh set rew ah gohsh) - The museum is at the end of this street, on the left.

These sentences are helpful when you need to give or follow more detailed directions.

Landmarks and Reference Points

Using landmarks is a great way to give or understand directions. Here are some common landmarks you might use:

Church - Une église (oon ay-gleez)

Bridge - Un pont (uhn pohn)

Park - Un parc (uhn park)

Statue - Une statue (oon stah-tew)

Fountain - Une fontaine (oon fon-ten)

You can combine these landmarks with direction phrases to give clear instructions. For example:

Le parc est à côté de l'église. (luh park eh ah koh-tay duh lay-gleez) - The park is next to the church.

Traversez le pont, puis tournez à gauche. (trah-ver-say luh pohn pwee toor-nay ah gohsh) - Cross the bridge, then turn left.

Using landmarks makes it easier for someone to follow your directions.

Talking About Distance

If you want to talk about how far away something is, you can use the following phrases:

Close - Près (preh)

Far - Loin (lwan)

About - À peu près (ah puh preh)

A few minutes - Quelques minutes (kel-kuh mee-nyoot)

A kilometer - Un kilomètre (uhn kee-loh-meh-tr)

Here are some examples:

C'est près d'ici. (seh preh dee-see) - It's close to here.

C'est loin du centre-ville. (seh lwan dew sahn-truh veel) - It's far from downtown.

C'est à peu près cinq minutes à pied. (seh ah puh preh sank mee-nyoot ah pyay) - It's about five minutes on foot.

La gare est à un kilomètre. (lah gar eh ah uhn kee-loh-meh-tr) - The train station is one kilometer away.

These phrases will help you describe distances when giving or receiving directions.

Key Points to Remember:

1. **Basic Directional Vocabulary**: Learn essential words like gauche (left), droit (right), tout droit (straight), and près de (near) to navigate and describe locations in French.

2. **Asking for Directions**: Use phrases like Où est...? (Where is...?) and Où sont...? (Where

are...?) to inquire about specific locations, such as Où est la banque? (Where is the bank?).

3. **Understanding Directions**: Familiarize yourself with common phrases like Allez tout droit (Go straight) and Tournez à gauche (Turn left) to follow directions effectively.

4. **Giving Directions**: Be prepared to help others with phrases like Allez tout droit, puis tournez à gauche (Go straight, then turn left) to guide them accurately.

5. **Using Landmarks and Describing Locations**: Combine landmarks like église (church) and pont (bridge) with directional phrases to give clear and precise instructions, such as Le parc est à côté de l'église (The park is next to the church).

Chapter 28

Transportation

In this chapter, we're going to learn about **Transportation** in French. Whether you're traveling in a city, taking a trip, or just getting around town, knowing how to talk about transportation is essential. By the end of this chapter, you'll be able to name different types of transportation, ask for directions, and talk about how you get from one place to another in French. Let's get started!

Basic Vocabulary for Transportation

Let's start by learning some common words for different types of transportation in French:

Car - Une voiture (oon vwah-tyoor)

Bus - Un bus (uhn boos)

Train - Un train (uhn tran)

Metro/Subway - Le métro (luh meh-troh)

Bicycle - Un vélo (uhn vay-loh)

Taxi - Un taxi (uhn tak-see)

Airplane - Un avion (uhn ah-vyon)

Boat - Un bateau (uhn bah-toh)

Motorcycle - Une moto (oon moh-toh)

Foot - À pied (ah pyay)

These words will help you talk about how you travel from one place to another. Now, let's learn how to talk about using these different types of transportation.

Talking About How You Travel

If you want to say how you're traveling, you can use the phrase Je vais en/à... (zhuh vay ahn/ah), which means "I'm going by/on...". Here's how you can use it with different types of transportation:

Je vais en voiture. (zhuh vay ahn vwah-tyoor) - I'm going by car.

Je vais en bus. (zhuh vay ahn boos) - I'm going by bus.

Je vais en train. (zhuh vay ahn tran) - I'm going by train.

Je vais en métro. (zhuh vay ahn meh-troh) - I'm going by metro/subway.

Je vais à pied. (zhuh vay ah pyay) - I'm going on foot.

You can also use the phrase Je prends... (zhuh prahn), which means "I'm taking...". For example:

Je prends le bus. (zhuh prahn luh boos) - I'm taking the bus.

Je prends le train. (zhuh prahn luh tran) - I'm taking the train.

Je prends un taxi. (zhuh prahn uhn tak-see) - I'm taking a taxi.

These phrases will help you explain how you're getting to your destination.

Asking About Transportation

When you're in a new place, you might need to ask about transportation options. Here's how you can ask in French:

Où est la gare? (oo eh lah gar) - Where is the train station?

Où est l'arrêt de bus? (oo eh la-ray duh boos) - Where is the bus stop?

Où est la station de métro? (oo eh lah stah-syon duh meh-troh) - Where is the metro station?

If you need to know when the next bus or train is coming, you can ask:

À quelle heure passe le prochain bus? (ah kel uhr pass luh proh-shan boos) - What time is the next bus?

À quelle heure part le prochain train? (ah kel uhr par luh proh-shan tran) - What time does the next train leave?

If you're asking for a ticket, you can say:

Je voudrais un billet pour... (zhuh voo-dray uhn bee-yay poor) - I would like a ticket for...

For example:

Je voudrais un billet pour Paris. (zhuh voo-dray uhn bee-yay poor pah-ree) - I would like a ticket for Paris.

Je voudrais un billet aller-retour. (zhuh voo-dray uhn bee-yay ah-lay ruh-toor) - I would like a round-trip ticket.

These questions will help you navigate transportation systems in French-speaking areas.

Understanding Transportation Signs

When you're traveling, you'll see many signs that help you find your way. Here are some common transportation-related signs in French:

Entrance - Entrée (ahn-tray)

Exit - Sortie (sor-tee)

Platform - Quai (kay)

Schedule - Horaire (oh-rair)

Tickets - Billets (bee-yay)

Ticket office - Guichet (gee-shay)

Departure - Départ (day-par)

Arrival - Arrivée (ah-ree-vay)

Knowing these words will help you understand the signs you see at train stations, airports, and bus stops.

Buying Tickets

If you're buying a ticket for a bus, train, or other transportation, here's how you can ask for one:

Je voudrais un billet pour Paris, s'il vous plaît. (zhuh voo-dray uhn bee-yay poor pah-ree, seel voo pleh) - I would like a ticket to Paris, please.

You can also specify if you want a one-way ticket or a round-trip ticket:

Un billet aller simple (uhn bee-yay ah-lay sampl) - A one-way ticket

Un billet aller-retour (uhn bee-yay ah-lay ruh-toor) - A round-trip ticket

If you want to ask how much the ticket costs, you can say:

Combien coûte un billet pour...? (kohm-byen koot uhn bee-yay poor) - How much is a ticket to...?

For example:

Combien coûte un billet pour Marseille? (kohm-byen koot uhn bee-yay poor mar-say) - How much is a ticket to Marseille?

These phrases will help you buy tickets and make your travel plans.

Talking About Your Travel Plans

If you want to talk about where you're going or how you're traveling, here are some phrases you can use:

Je vais à Paris en train. (zhuh vay ah pah-ree ahn tran) - I'm going to Paris by train.

Nous allons à l'aéroport en taxi. (noo zah-lon ah lay-oh-por ahn tak-see) - We're going to the airport by taxi.

Ils prennent le bus pour aller à l'école. (eel pren luh boos poor ah-lay ah lay-kohl) - They take the bus to go to school.

Je vais en vacances en avion. (zhuh vay ahn vah-kans ahn ah-vyon) - I'm going on vacation by airplane.

These sentences will help you explain your travel plans and how you're getting to your destination.

Talking About Travel Time

If you want to talk about how long a trip will take, you can use these phrases:

Le voyage dure deux heures. (luh vwoy-ahzh dur duh uhr) - The trip takes two hours.

Le vol dure trois heures. (luh vol dur trwa uhr) - The flight takes three hours.

Le trajet en bus dure trente minutes. (luh trah-zhay ahn boos dur trahnt mee-nyoot) - The bus ride takes thirty minutes.

If you want to ask someone how long it will take to get somewhere, you can say:

Combien de temps faut-il pour aller à...? (kohm-byen duh tahn foh-teel poor ah-lay ah) - How long does it take to get to...?

For example:

Combien de temps faut-il pour aller à la gare? (kohm-byen duh tahn foh-teel poor ah-lay ah lah gar) - How long does it take to get to the train station?

These phrases will help you talk about travel times and plan your trips.

Giving Directions Using Transportation

If someone asks you how to get somewhere using public transportation, here's how you can give directions:

Pour aller au musée, prenez le bus numéro 5. (poor ah-lay oh mew-zay pruh-nay luh boos noo-may-ro sank) - To get to the museum, take bus number 5.

Descendez à la station de métro Opéra. (day-sahn-day ah lah stah-syon duh meh-troh oh-pay-rah) - Get off at the Opéra metro station.

Vous pouvez prendre le train pour aller à Versailles. (voo poo-vay prahn-druh luh tran poor ah-lay ah ver-sigh) - You can take the train to go to Versailles.

These phrases will help you explain how to get to different places using public transportation.

Common Phrases for Traveling by Car

If you're traveling by car, here are some phrases you might find useful:

Nous allons en voiture. (noo zah-lon ahn vwah-tyoor) - We're going by car.

Je conduis jusqu'à la plage. (zhuh kon-dwee zhuhs-kah lah plahzh) - I'm driving to the beach.

Il y a beaucoup de circulation. (eel yah boh-koo duh seer-kyoo-lah-syon) - There's a lot of traffic.

Je dois faire le plein d'essence. (zhuh dwah fehr luh plan day-sahns) - I need to fill up with gas.

If you need to ask for directions while driving, you can say:

Comment va-t-on à...? (koh-mahn vah-tohn ah) - How do you get to...?

For example:

Comment va-t-on à l'aéroport? (koh-mahn vah-tohn ah lay-oh-por) - How do you get to the airport?

These phrases will help you if you're driving in a French-speaking area.

Talking About Tickets and Reservations

If you need to make a reservation or talk about tickets, here are some phrases you can use:

J'ai une réservation pour le train de 10 heures. (zhay oon ray-zair-vah-syon poor luh tran duh deez uhr) - I have a reservation for the 10 o'clock train.

Je voudrais annuler ma réservation. (zhuh voo-dray ah-nyoo-lay mah ray-zair-vah-syon) - I would like to cancel my reservation.

Où puis-je acheter des billets? (oo pweezh ah-shay-tay day bee-yay) - Where can I buy tickets?

Est-ce qu'il reste des places? (ess keel rest day plass) - Are there any seats left?

These phrases will help you handle tickets and reservations for your travel plans.

Key Points to Remember:

1. **Basic Transportation Vocabulary**: Familiarize yourself with essential transportation terms like voiture (car), bus (bus), train (train), métro (subway), and vélo (bicycle) to discuss how you travel.

2. **Talking About Travel Methods**: Use phrases like Je vais en/à… (I'm going by/on…) and Je prends… (I'm taking…) to explain your mode of transportation, such as Je vais en bus (I'm going by bus).

3. **Asking and Understanding Directions**: Learn to ask for directions with Où est…? (Where is…?) and understand common directional phrases like Allez tout droit (Go straight) and Tournez à gauche (Turn left).

4. **Buying Tickets**: Practice phrases like Je voudrais un billet pour… (I would like a ticket for…) and Combien coûte un billet pour…? (How much is a ticket to…?) to purchase tickets for your journey.

5. **Talking About Travel Time and Reservations**: Use phrases like Le voyage dure… (The trip takes…) to discuss travel times, and J'ai une réservation pour… (I have a reservation for…) to manage your travel reservations.

Chapter 29

Health and Body Parts

In this chapter, we're going to learn about **Health and Body Parts** in French. Knowing how to talk about your body and health is important, especially if you're not feeling well or need to describe a symptom to someone. By the end of this chapter, you'll be able to name different parts of the body in French, talk about common health issues, and describe how you're feeling. Let's get started!

Basic Vocabulary for Body Parts

First, let's learn the names of some common body parts in French. Here are the basics:

Head - La tête (lah tet)

Eye - Un œil (uhn uh-y) / Les yeux (lay z-yuh) for eyes

Nose - Le nez (luh nay)

Mouth - La bouche (lah boosh)

Ear - Une oreille (oon oh-ray) / Les oreilles (layz oh-ray) for ears

Arm - Le bras (luh brah)

Hand - La main (lah man)

Finger - Le doigt (luh dwah)

Leg - La jambe (lah zhamb)

Knee - Le genou (luh zhuh-noo)

Foot - Le pied (luh pyay)

Stomach - Le ventre (luh von-truh)

Back - Le dos (luh doh)

These words will help you describe different parts of your body in French. Now, let's learn how to talk about health and how you're feeling.

Talking About How You Feel

If you want to tell someone how you're feeling, you can use the verb se sentir (suh sahn-teer), which means "to feel." Here's how you can use it:

Je me sens bien. (zhuh muh sahn byan) - I feel good.

Je me sens mal. (zhuh muh sahn mal) - I feel bad.

Je me sens fatigué. (zhuh muh sahn fah-tee-gay) - I feel tired.

Je me sens malade. (zhuh muh sahn mah-lahd) - I feel sick.

These phrases will help you describe your general feelings. Now, let's get more specific.

Describing Pain or Discomfort

If you're feeling pain or discomfort in a specific part of your body, you can use the phrase J'ai mal à... (zhay mal ah), which means "I have pain in..." or "My...hurts." Here are some examples:

J'ai mal à la tête. (zhay mal ah lah tet) - I have a headache. (Literally: My head hurts.)

J'ai mal au dos. (zhay mal oh doh) - I have a backache. (Literally: My back hurts.)

J'ai mal au ventre. (zhay mal oh von-truh) - I have a stomachache. (Literally: My stomach hurts.)

J'ai mal aux dents. (zhay mal oh don) - I have a toothache. (Literally: My teeth hurt.)

J'ai mal à la gorge. (zhay mal ah lah gorzh) - I have a sore throat. (Literally: My throat hurts.)

If you're experiencing pain somewhere else, just replace the body part in the phrase J'ai mal à... with the appropriate word.

Talking About Common Health Issues

Now let's learn some phrases to describe common health issues or symptoms you might have:

Cold - Un rhume (uhn room)

Fever - Une fièvre (oon fee-evr)

Cough - Une toux (oon too)

Sore throat - Un mal de gorge (uhn mal duh gorzh)

Stomachache - Un mal de ventre (uhn mal duh von-truh)

Headache - Un mal de tête (uhn mal duh tet)

Here's how you can use these words in sentences:

J'ai un rhume. (zhay uhn room) - I have a cold.

J'ai de la fièvre. (zhay duh lah fee-evr) - I have a fever.

J'ai une toux. (zhay oon too) - I have a cough.

J'ai un mal de gorge. (zhay uhn mal duh gorzh) - I have a sore throat.

J'ai un mal de tête. (zhay uhn mal duh tet) - I have a headache.

These phrases will help you describe how you're feeling if you're not well.

Going to the Doctor

If you need to go to the doctor, it's important to know how to explain what's wrong. Here are some useful phrases:

Je voudrais prendre rendez-vous avec le médecin. (zhuh voo-dray prahn-druh rahn-day-voo ah-vek luh med-sahn) - I would like to make an appointment with the doctor.

J'ai besoin de voir un médecin. (zhay buh-zwahn duh vwar uhn med-sahn) - I need to see a doctor.

Où est la pharmacie la plus proche? (oo eh lah far-mah-see lah ploo prohsh) - Where is the nearest pharmacy?

At the doctor's office, you might be asked to describe your symptoms. You can use the phrases we've already learned to do this, such as J'ai mal à... or Je me sens....

If the doctor prescribes medication, they might give you instructions like:

Prenez ce médicament trois fois par jour. (pruh-nay suh may-dee-kah-mahn trwa fwah par zhoor) - Take this medicine three times a day.

Reposez-vous et buvez beaucoup d'eau. (ruh-poh-zay voo eh bew-vay boh-koo doh) - Rest and drink plenty of water.

Understanding these instructions is important for following the doctor's advice.

Staying Healthy

To talk about staying healthy or general health habits, here are some useful phrases:

Je fais du sport. (zhuh feh dew spor) - I exercise. (Literally: I do sports.)

Je mange des fruits et des légumes. (zhuh mahnzh day frwee ay day lay-gum) - I eat fruits and vegetables.

Je bois beaucoup d'eau. (zhuh bwah boh-koo doh) - I drink a lot of water.

Je dors huit heures par nuit. (zhuh dor wheat uhr par nwee) - I sleep eight hours per night.

These habits can help you talk about how you take care of your health.

Asking How Someone Else Feels

If you want to ask someone else how they're feeling, you can say:

Comment te sens-tu? (koh-mahn tuh sahn tew) - How do you feel?

Tu te sens bien? (tew tuh sahn byan) - Do you feel well?

Est-ce que ça va? (ess kuh sah vah) - Are you okay?

If someone tells you they're not feeling well, you can respond with:

Je suis désolé. (zhuh swee day-zoh-lay) - I'm sorry to hear that.

Prends soin de toi. (prahns swan duh twah) - Take care of yourself.

These phrases can help you show concern for someone else's health.

Talking About Allergies

If you have allergies, it's important to be able to talk about them in French. Here's how:

Allergy - Une allergie (oon ah-ler-zhee)

I'm allergic to... - Je suis allergique à... (zhuh swee ah-ler-zheek ah)

For example:

Je suis allergique aux arachides. (zhuh swee ah-ler-zheek ohz ah-rah-sheed) - I'm allergic to peanuts.

Je suis allergique au pollen. (zhuh swee ah-ler-zheek oh poh-len) - I'm allergic to pollen.

Knowing how to talk about your allergies is important for staying safe, especially when traveling or eating out.

Emergency Phrases

In case of an emergency, here are some phrases you should know:

J'ai besoin d'aide! (zhay buh-zwahn ded) - I need help!

Appelez une ambulance! (ahp-lay oon ahm-byoo-lahns) - Call an ambulance!

Il y a un accident. (eel yah uhn aks-ee-dahn) - There's been an accident.

Je suis blessé(e). (zhuh swee blay-say/blay-say) - I'm injured.

These phrases can be crucial in an emergency situation.

Key Points to Remember:

1. **Basic Vocabulary for Body Parts**: Learn essential body part names like la tête (head), le bras (arm), la jambe (leg), and le ventre (stomach) to describe different parts of your body in French.

2. **Talking About How You Feel**: Use phrases like Je me sens bien (I feel good) and Je me sens malade (I feel sick) to express how you're feeling.

3. **Describing Pain or Discomfort**: Express pain using J'ai mal à… (I have pain in…), such as J'ai mal à la tête (I have a headache) or J'ai mal au dos (I have a backache).

4. **Talking About Common Health Issues**: Be able to describe common health problems with phrases like J'ai un rhume (I have a cold) and J'ai de la fièvre (I have a fever).

5. **Going to the Doctor**: Know how to make a doctor's appointment and describe your symptoms with phrases like Je voudrais prendre rendez-vous avec le médecin (I would like to make an appointment with the doctor) and J'ai besoin de voir un médecin (I need to see a doctor).

Chapter 30

Animals and Nature

In this chapter, we're going to learn about **Animals and Nature** in French. Whether you love animals or enjoy spending time outdoors, knowing how to talk about the natural world is important. By the end of this chapter, you'll be able to name different animals, talk about nature, and describe your experiences with the environment in French. Let's begin!

Basic Vocabulary for Animals

Let's start by learning the names of some common animals in French. Here are some that you might already know:

Dog - Un chien (uhn shyan)

Cat - Un chat (uhn shah)

Bird - Un oiseau (uhn wah-zoh)

Fish - Un poisson (uhn pwah-son)

Horse - Un cheval (uhn shuh-val)

Rabbit - Un lapin (uhn lah-pan)

Turtle - Une tortue (oon tor-tew)

Frog - Une grenouille (oon gruh-nwee)

These words will help you talk about some of the animals you might see in your daily life. Now let's learn how to talk about wild animals.

Wild Animals

Wild animals are those that live in the forests, jungles, oceans, and other natural habitats. Here are some common wild animals in French:

Lion - Un lion (uhn lyohn)

Tiger - Un tigre (uhn tee-gruh)

Elephant - Un éléphant (uhn ay-lay-fahn)

Bear - Un ours (uhn oors)

Wolf - Un loup (uhn loo)

Giraffe - Une girafe (oon zhee-raf)

Monkey - Un singe (uhn sanj)

Dolphin - Un dauphin (uhn doh-fan)

These animals are often seen in zoos or documentaries, but they are also found in their natural environments around the world.

Talking About Pets

Many people have pets, or animaux de compagnie (ah-nee-moh duh kohm-pah-nee), which are animals that live with us at home. Here's how to talk about pets in French:

J'ai un chien. (zhay uhn shyan) - I have a dog.

J'ai un chat. (zhay uhn shah) - I have a cat.

J'ai un poisson rouge. (zhay uhn pwah-son roozh) - I have a goldfish.

J'ai deux oiseaux. (zhay duh wah-zoh) - I have two birds.

If you want to ask someone if they have a pet, you can say:

Est-ce que tu as un animal de compagnie? (ess kuh tew ah uhn ah-nee-mal duh kohm-pah-nee) - Do you have a pet?

Talking about pets is a great way to connect with others, especially if you both love animals!

Talking About Farm Animals

Farm animals, or animaux de la ferme (ah-nee-moh duh lah fehrm), are animals that live on farms and are often raised for food or other resources. Here are some common farm animals in French:

Cow - Une vache (oon vash)

Chicken - Une poule (oon pool)

Sheep - Un mouton (uhn moo-ton)

Pig - Un cochon (uhn koh-shon)

Goat - Une chèvre (oon shevr)

Duck - Un canard (uhn kah-nar)

Horse - Un cheval (uhn shuh-val)

If you want to say that you visited a farm or saw these animals, you could say:

J'ai visité une ferme et j'ai vu des vaches, des moutons et des poules. (zhay vee-zee-tay oon fehrm ay zhay voo day vash, day moo-ton ay day pool) - I visited a farm and saw cows, sheep, and chickens.

These phrases will help you describe your experiences with farm animals in French.

Basic Vocabulary for Nature

Now that we've learned about animals, let's talk about nature. Here are some basic words related to nature in French:

Tree - Un arbre (uhn arbr)

Flower - Une fleur (oon flur)

Forest - Une forêt (oon for-ay)

Mountain - Une montagne (oon mon-tan-yuh)

River - Une rivière (oon ree-vyehr)

Lake - Un lac (uhn lak)

Ocean - Un océan (uhn oh-say-ahn)

Beach - Une plage (oon plahzh)

Sky - Le ciel (luh syehl)

These words will help you describe the natural world around you, whether you're talking about a hike in the mountains or a day at the beach.

Talking About the Weather

The weather, or le temps (luh tahn), is a big part of nature. Here are some ways to talk about the weather in French:

It's sunny - Il fait du soleil (eel feh dew soh-lay)

It's raining - Il pleut (eel pleuh)

It's snowing - Il neige (eel nezh)

It's windy - Il fait du vent (eel feh dew vahn)

It's cloudy - Il fait nuageux (eel feh nweh-zhuh)

If you want to ask someone about the weather, you can say:

Quel temps fait-il? (kel tahn feh-teel) - What's the weather like?

To describe the weather where you are, you can say:

Il fait beau aujourd'hui. (eel feh boh oh-zhoor-dwee) - The weather is nice today.

Il fait mauvais aujourd'hui. (eel feh moh-veh oh-zhoor-dwee) - The weather is bad today.

Talking about the weather is a great way to start a conversation, especially when you're outdoors.

Describing Natural Landscapes

If you want to describe the natural landscapes you see, here are some useful phrases:

La montagne est très haute. (lah mon-tan-yuh eh treh oht) - The mountain is very tall.

La forêt est dense. (lah for-ay eh dahns) - The forest is dense.

Le lac est calme et beau. (luh lak eh kahlm ay boh) - The lake is calm and beautiful.

La plage est pleine de sable fin. (lah plahzh eh plehn duh sahbl fan) - The beach is full of fine sand.

If you're talking about a trip you took in nature, you might say:

J'ai fait une randonnée dans la montagne. (zhay feh oon rahn-doh-nay dahn lah mon-tan-yuh) - I went hiking in the mountains.

Nous avons campé près de la rivière. (noo zah-von kahm-pay preh duh lah ree-vyehr) - We camped near the river.

These phrases will help you describe your experiences in nature and share them with others.

Talking About Environmental Issues

Caring for the environment, or l'environnement (lahn-vee-rohn-mahn), is important. Here are some phrases to talk about environmental issues in French:

Il faut protéger la nature. (eel foh proh-tay-zhay lah nah-tyoor) - We must protect nature.

Le réchauffement climatique est un problème sérieux. (luh ray-shohf-mahn klee-mah-teek eh uhn proh-blehm seh-ryuh) - Climate change is a serious problem.

Nous devons réduire la pollution. (noo duh-von ray-dweer lah poh-loo-syon) - We must reduce pollution.

These phrases can help you talk about the importance of protecting the environment and what we can do to help.

Key Points to Remember:

1. **Basic Vocabulary for Animals**: Learn the names of common animals like chien (dog), chat (cat), and oiseau (bird) to talk about your favorite animals in French.

2. **Talking About Wild and Farm Animals**: Use phrases to describe wild animals like lion (lion) and farm animals like vache (cow) in French, which are essential for conversations about nature and farms.

3. **Talking About Pets**: Express whether you have pets with phrases like J'ai un chien (I have a dog) or ask others Est-ce que tu as un animal de compagnie? (Do you have a pet?).

4. **Basic Vocabulary for Nature**: Learn nature-related words such as arbre (tree), montagne (mountain), and rivière (river) to describe your surroundings in French.

5. **Talking About the Weather**: Discuss weather conditions with phrases like Il fait du soleil (It's sunny) and Il pleut (It's raining), which are useful for daily conversations.

Chapter 31

School and Education

In this chapter, we're going to learn about **School and Education** in French. School is a big part of your life, and knowing how to talk about it in French will help you discuss your daily routines, subjects, and what you enjoy or find challenging. By the end of this chapter, you'll be able to name different school subjects, talk about your school day, and describe your experiences in education. Let's get started!

Basic Vocabulary for School

Let's begin by learning some basic words related to school in French:

School - L'école (lay-kohl)

Classroom - La salle de classe (lah sal duh klass)

Teacher - Le professeur (luh pro-fess-eur) or Le maître/la maîtresse (luh meh-truh/lah meh-tress) for younger students

Student - L'élève (lay-lev)

Lesson - La leçon (lah luh-son)

Homework - Les devoirs (lay duh-vwahr)

Exam - L'examen (lex-zah-men)

Recess - La récréation (lah ray-kray-ah-syon)

Lunch - Le déjeuner (luh day-zhuh-nay)

Library - La bibliothèque (lah bee-blee-oh-tek)

Gym - Le gymnase (luh zheem-nahz)

These words will help you describe your school environment and talk about your daily activities. Now let's move on to school subjects.

School Subjects

In school, you learn different subjects, or matières (mah-tyehr). Here are some common school subjects in French:

Math - Les mathématiques (lay mah-tay-mah-teek) or les maths (lay mats) for short

Science - Les sciences (lay see-ahns)

History - L'histoire (lees-twahr)

Geography - La géographie (lah zhay-oh-grah-fee)

English - L'anglais (lahng-glay)

French - Le français (luh frahn-say)

Art - L'art (lar)

Physical Education (PE) - L'éducation physique (lay-doo-kah-syon fee-zeek)

Music - La musique (lah mew-zeek)

If you want to talk about what subjects you like or dislike, you can use the phrase J'aime... (zhem) for "I like..." and Je n'aime pas... (zhuh nem pah) for "I don't like..." Here are some examples:

J'aime les mathématiques. (zhem lay mah-tay-mah-teek) - I like math.

Je n'aime pas l'histoire. (zhuh nem pah lees-twahr) - I don't like history.

J'aime la musique. (zhem lah mew-zeek) - I like music.

Je n'aime pas la géographie. (zhuh nem pah lah zhay-oh-grah-fee) - I don't like geography.

These phrases will help you express your preferences about different school subjects.

Talking About Your School Day

Your school day, or journée scolaire (zhoor-nay skoh-lehr), is filled with different activities. Here's how you can talk about your typical school day in French:

Je vais à l'école à huit heures. (zhuh vay ah lay-kohl ah weet uhr) - I go to school at eight o'clock.

J'ai cours de français à neuf heures. (zhay koor duh frahn-say ah nuhf uhr) - I have French class at nine o'clock.

La récréation commence à dix heures et demie. (lah ray-kray-ah-syon koh-mahnss ah dees uhr ay duh-mee) - Recess starts at ten thirty.

Nous déjeunons à midi. (noo day-zhoo-non ah mee-dee) - We have lunch at noon.

Je rentre à la maison à trois heures et quart. (zhuh rahntr ah lah may-zon ah trwa uhr ay kar) - I go home at three fifteen.

If you want to ask a classmate about their school day, you can say:

À quelle heure commence ton premier cours? (ah kel uhr koh-mahnss ton pruh-mee-ayr koor) - What time does your first class start?

Qu'est-ce que tu as après la récréation? (kes-kuh tew ah ah-pray lah ray-kray-ah-syon) - What do you have after recess?

These phrases will help you talk about your schedule and daily routine at school.

Talking About Homework and Exams

Homework, or les devoirs (lay duh-vwahr), and exams, or les examens (layg-zah-men), are a big part of school. Here's how to talk about them in French:

J'ai beaucoup de devoirs ce soir. (zhay boh-koo duh duh-vwahr suh swahr) - I have a lot of homework tonight.

Je dois faire mes devoirs avant le dîner. (zhuh dwah fehr may duh-vwahr ah-vahn luh dee-nay) - I have to do my homework before dinner.

Il y a un examen de maths demain. (eel yah uhn layg-zah-men duh mats duh-man) - There's a math exam tomorrow.

Je suis nerveux/nerveuse à cause de l'examen. (zhuh swee nair-vuh/nair-vuhz ah koze duh layg-zah-men) - I'm nervous because of the exam.

If you want to ask someone about their homework or exams, you can say:

As-tu fait tes devoirs? (ah tew feh tay duh-vwahr) - Did you do your homework?

Es-tu prêt(e) pour l'examen? (ess tew preh/praht poor layg-zah-men) - Are you ready for the exam?

These phrases will help you talk about your assignments and tests in French.

Talking About Your Favorite Classes

If you have a favorite class, here's how you can talk about it in French:

Ma classe préférée est l'art. (mah klass pray-fay-ray eh lar) - My favorite class is art.

J'adore les sciences parce que c'est intéressant. (zhah-dor lay see-ahns parss kuh say an-tay-ray-sahn) - I love science because it's interesting.

Le français est ma matière préférée. (luh frahn-say eh mah mah-tyehr pray-fay-ray) - French is my favorite subject.

Je trouve l'histoire fascinante. (zhuh troov lees-twahr fah-see-nahnt) - I find history fascinating.

If you want to ask someone about their favorite class, you can say:

Quelle est ta matière préférée? (kel eh tah mah-tyehr pray-fay-ray) - What's your favorite subject?

Pourquoi aimes-tu cette classe? (poor-kwah em tew set klass) - Why do you like this class?

These phrases will help you express your preferences and ask others about theirs.

Talking About Your School Experiences

If you want to talk about your experiences at school, here are some phrases you can use:

J'aime bien l'école parce que j'apprends beaucoup de choses. (zhem byan lay-kohl parss kuh zhah-pron boh-koo duh shohz) - I like school because I learn a lot of things.

Mon école est grande et moderne. (mon lay-kohl eh grahnd ay moh-dairn) - My school is big and modern.

J'ai des amis formidables à l'école. (zhay dayz ah-mee for-mee-dah-bl ah lay-kohl) - I have great friends at school.

Les professeurs sont gentils et toujours prêts à aider. (lay pro-fess-eur sohn zhahn-tee ay too-zhoor preh ah ay-day) - The teachers are kind and always ready to help.

If you want to ask someone about their school experiences, you can say:

Comment est ton école? (koh-mahn eh ton lay-kohl) - What's your school like?

Aimes-tu ton école? (em tew ton lay-kohl) - Do you like your school?

These phrases will help you talk about your school experiences and learn about others' experiences.

Talking About Extracurricular Activities

Extracurricular activities, or les activités extrascolaires (layz ak-tee-vee-tay ex-trah-skoh-lehr), are activities you do outside of regular classes. Here's how to talk about them in French:

Je fais partie du club de théâtre. (zhuh feh par-tee dew kluhb duh tay-ah-tr) - I'm part of the drama club.

Je joue au basketball après l'école. (zhuh zhway oh bas-ket-bol ah-pray lay-kohl) - I play basketball after school.

Je participe à l'orchestre de l'école. (zhuh par-tee-see-pah ah lor-kest-ruh duh lay-kohl) - I participate in the school orchestra.

Je suis membre du club de sciences. (zhuh swee mahm-br duh kluhb duh see-ahns) - I'm a member of the science club.

If you want to ask someone about their extracurricular activities, you can say:

Fais-tu partie d'un club? (feh tew par-tee duh-n kluhb) - Are you part of a club?

Que fais-tu après l'école? (kuh feh tew ah-pray lay-kohl) - What do you do after school?

These phrases will help you talk about your activities outside of regular classes and ask others about theirs.

Key Points to Remember:

1. **Basic School Vocabulary**: Learn essential French words like l'école (school), le professeur (teacher), and les devoirs (homework) to talk about your school environment and daily activities.

2. **Discussing School Subjects**: Express your preferences with phrases like J'aime les mathématiques (I like math) or Je n'aime pas l'histoire (I don't like history) to talk about different subjects.

3. **Describing Your School Day**: Use phrases such as Je vais à l'école à huit heures (I go to school at eight o'clock) to describe your daily routine and ask classmates about theirs.

4. **Talking About Homework and Exams**: Discuss your assignments and exams with phrases like J'ai beaucoup de devoirs ce soir (I have a lot of homework tonight) or Es-tu prêt pour l'examen? (Are you ready for the exam?).

5. **Extracurricular Activities**: Share your interests outside of class with phrases like Je fais partie du club de théâtre (I'm part of the drama club) and ask others about their

activities with Fais-tu partie d'un club? (Are you part of a club?).

Chapter 32

Work and Office Vocabulary

In this chapter, we're going to learn about **Work and Office Vocabulary** in French. Understanding the language of the workplace is important because it helps you talk about what adults do during the day, and it gives you an idea of what it might be like when you have a job in the future. By the end of this chapter, you'll be able to name different professions, talk about common tasks in an office, and understand basic work-related vocabulary in French. Let's get started!

Basic Vocabulary for Work

First, let's learn some common words related to work and the office in French:

Work/Job - Le travail (luh trah-vahy)

Office - Le bureau (luh byoo-roh)

Boss - Le patron / La patronne (luh pah-tron / lah pah-tronn)

Employee - L'employé(e) (lahm-plwah-yay / lahm-plwah-yay)

Colleague - Le collègue / La collègue (luh koh-lehg / lah koh-lehg)

Meeting - La réunion (lah ray-yoo-nyon)

Task - La tâche (lah tahsh)

Computer - L'ordinateur (lor-dee-nah-teur)

Email - Le courriel (luh koor-ryel) or Le mail (luh mel)

Phone - Le téléphone (luh tay-lay-fohn)

Document - Le document (luh doh-koo-mahn)

Printer - L'imprimante (lam-pree-mahnt)

Photocopier - La photocopieuse (lah foh-toh-koh-pyuhz)

These words will help you talk about the tools and places involved in work. Now let's move on to professions.

Common Professions

There are many different types of jobs that people do. Here are some common professions in French:

Teacher - Le professeur / La professeure (luh pro-fess-eur / lah pro-fess-eur)

Doctor - Le médecin (luh med-sahn)

Engineer - L'ingénieur / L'ingénieure (lan-zhay-nyur / lan-zhay-nyur)

Nurse - L'infirmier / L'infirmière (lan-feer-my-ay / lan-feer-my-ehr)

Lawyer - L'avocat / L'avocate (lah-voh-kah / lah-voh-kaht)

Accountant - Le comptable / La comptable (luh kohm-tah-bl / lah kohm-tah-bl)

Secretary - Le secrétaire / La secrétaire (luh suh-kre-tehr / lah suh-kre-tehr)

Chef - Le chef cuisinier / La chef cuisinière (luh shehf kwee-zeen-yay / lah shehf kwee-zeen-yair)

Artist - L'artiste (lar-teest)

If you want to say what someone does for a living, you can use the phrase Il/Elle est... (eel/ell eh), which means "He/She is...". For example:

Il est médecin. (eel eh med-sahn) - He is a doctor.

Elle est professeure. (ell eh pro-fess-eur) - She is a teacher.

Mon père est ingénieur. (mohn pehr eh zan-zhay-nyur) - My dad is an engineer.

Ma mère est avocate. (mah mehr eh ah-voh-kaht) - My mom is a lawyer.

These phrases will help you talk about different jobs and what people do for work.

Talking About Office Tasks

In an office, there are many tasks, or tâches (tahsh), that people do every day. Here are some common tasks in French:

To work on a project - Travailler sur un projet (trah-vah-yay soor uhn pro-zhay)

To send an email - Envoyer un courriel (ahn-vwah-yay uhn koor-ryel)

To answer the phone - Répondre au téléphone (ray-pondr oh tay-lay-fohn)

To write a report - Rédiger un rapport (ray-dee-zhay uhn rah-por)

To print a document - Imprimer un document (am-pree-may uhn doh-koo-mahn)

To organize a meeting - Organiser une réunion (or-gah-nee-zay oon ray-yoo-nyon)

To make a photocopy - Faire une photocopie (fehr oon foh-toh-koh-pee)

Here are some sentences using these phrases:

Je travaille sur un projet important. (zhuh trah-vah-yay soor uhn pro-zhay ahm-por-tahn) - I'm working on an important project.

Elle envoie un courriel à son collègue. (ell ahn-vwah uhn koor-ryel ah sohn koh-lehg) - She's sending an email to her colleague.

Nous organisons une réunion demain matin. (noo zor-gah-nee-zon oon ray-yoo-nyon duh-man mah-tan) - We're organizing a meeting tomorrow morning.

If you want to ask someone about their work tasks, you can say:

Sur quel projet travailles-tu? (soor kel pro-zhay trah-vahy tew) - What project are you working on?

As-tu imprimé le document? (ah tew am-pree-may luh doh-koo-mahn) - Did you print the document?

These phrases will help you describe common office tasks and ask others about their work.

Talking About Office Equipment

There's a lot of equipment in an office that helps people do their jobs. Here's how to talk about some of it in French:

Computer - L'ordinateur (lor-dee-nah-teur)

Printer - L'imprimante (lam-pree-mahnt)

Photocopier - La photocopieuse (lah foh-toh-koh-pyuhz)

Phone - Le téléphone (luh tay-lay-fohn)

Desk - Le bureau (luh byoo-roh)

Chair - La chaise (lah shehz)

File cabinet - Le classeur (luh klah-seur)

Here are some sentences using these words:

Je travaille à mon bureau avec mon ordinateur. (zhuh trah-vah-yay ah mohn byoo-roh ah-vek mohn lor-dee-nah-teur) - I work at my desk with my computer.

Il faut imprimer ce document avant la réunion. (eel foh am-pree-may suh doh-koo-mahn ah-vahn lah ray-yoo-nyon) - We need to print this document before the meeting.

Elle range les dossiers dans le classeur. (ell rahnzh lay doh-syay dahn luh klah-seur) - She files the documents in the file cabinet.

If you want to ask someone about office equipment, you can say:

Où est l'imprimante? (oo eh lam-pree-mahnt) - Where is the printer?

Peux-tu répondre au téléphone? (puh tew ray-pondr oh tay-lay-fohn) - Can you answer the phone?

These phrases will help you talk about the tools used in an office and ask others where things are or how to use them.

Talking About Work Schedules

Work schedules, or horaires de travail (ohr-ehr duh trah-vahy), are important in any job. Here's how to talk about them in French:

Full-time - À plein temps (ah plehn tahn)

Part-time - À temps partiel (ah tahn par-syel)

Morning shift - Le quart du matin (luh kar dew mah-tan)

Evening shift - Le quart du soir (luh kar dew swahr)

Overtime - Heures supplémentaires (uhr soo-play-men-tair)

Here are some sentences using these words:

Il travaille à plein temps dans un bureau. (eel trah-vah-yay ah plehn tahn dahn uhn byoo-roh) - He works full-time in an office.

Elle fait des heures supplémentaires cette semaine. (ell feh dayz uhr soo-play-men-tair set suh-men) - She's working overtime this week.

Je travaille le quart du soir. (zhuh trah-vah-yay luh kar dew swahr) - I work the evening shift.

If you want to ask someone about their work schedule, you can say:

Tu travailles à plein temps ou à temps partiel? (tew trah-vahy ah plehn tahn oo ah tahn par-syel) - Do you work full-time or part-time?

Quels sont tes horaires de travail? (kel sohn tayz ohr-ehr duh trah-vahy) - What are your work hours?

These phrases will help you talk about work schedules and understand how others organize their workday.

Talking About Workplaces

People work in many different places, or lieux de travail (lyuh duh trah-vahy). Here's how to talk about some common workplaces in French:

Office - Le bureau (luh byoo-roh)

Factory - L'usine (lew-zeen)

School - L'école (lay-kohl)

Hospital - L'hôpital (loh-pee-tahl)

Store - Le magasin (luh mah-gah-zan)

Restaurant - Le restaurant (luh res-toh-rahnt)

Here are some sentences using these words:

Elle travaille dans un bureau en ville. (ell trah-vah-yay dahn uhn byoo-roh ahn veel) - She works in an office in the city.

Il est médecin à l'hôpital. (eel eh med-sahn ah loh-pee-tahl) - He is a doctor at the hospital.

Mon père travaille dans une usine. (mohn pehr trah-vah-yay dahn oon lew-zeen) - My dad works in a factory.

If you want to ask someone where they work, you can say:

Où travailles-tu? (oo trah-vahy tew) - Where do you work?

Quel est ton lieu de travail? (kel eh ton lyuh duh trah-vahy) - What is your workplace?

These phrases will help you talk about different workplaces and ask others where they work.

Key Points to Remember:

1. **Basic Work Vocabulary**: Learn essential terms like le travail (work/job), le bureau (office), and le patron/la patronne (boss) to describe the workplace environment and roles.

2. **Common Professions**: Use phrases like Il est médecin (He is a doctor) and Elle est professeure (She is a teacher) to talk about different jobs and what people do for a living.

3. **Office Tasks**: Familiarize yourself with tasks like travailler sur un projet (to work on a project) and envoyer un courriel (to send an email) to discuss daily office activities.

4. **Work Schedules**: Understand and talk about different work schedules using terms like à plein temps (full-time) and heures supplémentaires (overtime).

5. **Workplaces**: Describe where people work using phrases like Il travaille dans une usine (He works in a factory) or Elle travaille dans un bureau (She works in an office).

Chapter 33

House and Home

In this chapter, we're going to learn about **House and Home** in French. Knowing how to talk about your house and the things inside it is important because it helps you describe where you live and the different rooms and objects around you. By the end of this chapter, you'll be able to name different rooms, describe your home, and talk about common household items in French. Let's get started!

Basic Vocabulary for the House

Let's start by learning some basic words related to the house in French:

House - La maison (lah may-zon)

Apartment - L'appartement (lah-par-tuh-mahn)

Room - La pièce (lah pyess)

Door - La porte (lah port)

Window - La fenêtre (lah fuh-netr)

Floor - Le sol (luh sohl)

Wall - Le mur (luh myur)

Ceiling - Le plafond (luh plah-fon)

Stairs - L'escalier (les-kah-lyay)

These words will help you describe the structure of your house or apartment. Now let's learn about the different rooms in a house.

Rooms in a House

Every house or apartment has different rooms, or pièces (pyess). Here are some common rooms you'll find in a home, along with their French names:

Living room - Le salon (luh sah-lon)

Kitchen - La cuisine (lah kwee-zeen)

Bedroom - La chambre (lah shom-br)

Bathroom - La salle de bain (lah sal duh ban)

Dining room - La salle à manger (lah sal ah mon-zhay)

Office - Le bureau (luh byoo-roh)

Garage - Le garage (luh gah-rahzh)

Garden - Le jardin (luh zhar-dan)

If you want to describe your home, you can use the following sentences:

Ma maison a trois chambres et un grand salon. (mah may-zon ah trwa shom-br ay uhn grahn sah-lon) - My house has three bedrooms and a big living room.

J'habite dans un appartement avec une petite cuisine. (zhah-beet dahn uhn ah-par-tuh-mahn ah-vek oon puh-teet kwee-zeen) - I live in an apartment with a small kitchen.

Il y a un jardin derrière la maison. (eel yah uhn zhar-dan deh-ree-ehr lah may-zon) - There's a garden behind the house.

If you want to ask someone about their home, you can say:

Combien de chambres y a-t-il dans ta maison? (kohm-byen duh shom-br yah-teel dahn tah may-zon) - How many bedrooms are there in your house?

Est-ce que ta maison a un garage? (ess kuh tah may-zon ah uhn gah-rahzh) - Does your house have a garage?

These phrases will help you talk about the rooms in your house and ask others about theirs.

Common Household Items

Now that we've learned about the rooms in a house, let's talk about some common household items you might find in each room. Here are some examples:

In the living room:

Sofa - Le canapé (luh kah-nah-pay)

Television - La télévision (lah tay-lay-vee-zyon)

Coffee table - La table basse (lah tah-bl bahss)

Rug - Le tapis (luh tah-pee)

In the kitchen:

Refrigerator - Le réfrigérateur (luh ray-free-zhay-rah-teur)

Oven - Le four (luh fohr)

Stove - La cuisinière (lah kwee-zeen-yair)

Sink - L'évier (lay-vyay)

In the bedroom:

Bed - Le lit (luh lee)

Wardrobe/Closet - L'armoire (lar-mwar)

Dresser - La commode (lah koh-mod)

Desk - Le bureau (luh byoo-roh)

In the bathroom:

Shower - La douche (lah doosh)

Bathtub - La baignoire (lah behn-wahr)

Toilet - Les toilettes (lay twah-let)

Sink - Le lavabo (luh lah-vah-boh)

Here are some sentences using these words:

Je regarde la télévision dans le salon. (zhuh ruh-gard lah tay-lay-vee-zyon dahn luh sah-lon) - I watch TV in the living room.

La cuisine a un grand réfrigérateur et un four moderne. (lah kwee-zeen ah uhn grahn ray-free-zhay-rah-teur ay uhn fohr moh-dairn) - The kitchen has a large refrigerator and a modern oven.

Ma chambre a un lit confortable et une grande armoire. (mah shom-br ah uhn lee kohn-for-tah-bl ay oon grahnd ar-mwar) - My bedroom has a comfortable bed and a large wardrobe.

If you want to ask someone about the items in their home, you can say:

Est-ce que ta chambre a un bureau? (ess kuh tah shom-br ah uhn byoo-roh) - Does your bedroom have a desk?

Où est le réfrigérateur dans la cuisine? (oo eh luh ray-free-zhay-rah-teur dahn lah kwee-zeen) - Where is the refrigerator in the kitchen?

These phrases will help you describe the items in your home and ask others about theirs.

Talking About House Chores

House chores, or les tâches ménagères (lay tahsh may-nah-zhehr), are the things you do to keep your home clean and organized. Here are some common chores in French:

To clean - Nettoyer (nay-twah-yay)

To cook - Cuisiner (kwee-zee-nay)

To do the dishes - Faire la vaisselle (fehr lah vay-sell)

To do the laundry - Faire la lessive (fehr lah lay-seev)

To take out the trash - Sortir la poubelle (sor-teer lah poo-bell)

To vacuum - Passer l'aspirateur (pah-say lah-speer-ah-teur)

Here are some sentences using these words:

Je nettoie ma chambre le samedi. (zhuh nay-twah mah shom-br luh sahm-dee) - I clean my room on Saturdays.

Mon frère fait la vaisselle après le dîner. (mohn frair fehr lah vay-sell ah-pray luh dee-nay) - My brother does the dishes after dinner.

Nous faisons la lessive le dimanche. (noo feh-zon lah lay-seev luh dee-mahnsh) - We do the laundry on Sundays.

If you want to ask someone about their house chores, you can say:

Est-ce que tu fais la vaisselle? (ess kuh tew fehr lah vay-sell) - Do you do the dishes?

Quand fais-tu le ménage? (kahn feh-tew luh may-nazh) - When do you clean the house?

These phrases will help you talk about the chores you do at home and ask others about theirs.

Talking About Where You Live

If you want to talk about where you live, here are some useful phrases in French:

J'habite dans une maison à la campagne. (zhah-beet dahn oon may-zon ah lah kahn-pah-nye) - I live in a house in the countryside.

Nous habitons dans un appartement en ville. (noo zah-bee-ton dahn uhn ah-par-tuh-mahn ahn veel) - We live in an apartment in the city.

Ma maison est près de l'école. (mah may-zon eh preh duh lay-kohl) - My house is near the school.

If you want to ask someone about where they live, you can say:

Où habites-tu? (oo ah-beet tew) - Where do you live?

Est-ce que tu habites en ville ou à la campagne? (ess kuh tew ah-beet ahn veel oo ah lah kahn-pah-nye) - Do you live in the city or in the countryside?

These phrases will help you describe your home's location and ask others about where they live.

Key Points to Remember:

1. **Basic House Vocabulary**: Learn essential terms like la maison (house), l'appartement (apartment), and la pièce (room) to describe the structure and spaces in your home.

2. **Rooms in a House**: Familiarize yourself with common room names like le salon (living room), la cuisine (kitchen), and la chambre (bedroom) to talk about different parts of your home.

3. **Common Household Items**: Understand key items in different rooms, such as le canapé (sofa) in the living room, le réfrigérateur (refrigerator) in the kitchen, and le lit (bed) in the bedroom, to describe what's inside your home.

4. **House Chores**: Learn how to talk about daily chores with phrases like faire la vaisselle (do the dishes) and passer l'aspirateur (vacuum) to discuss household responsibilities.

5. **Talking About Where You Live**: Use phrases like J'habite dans une maison (I live in a house) or Nous habitons en ville (We live in the city) to describe your living situation and ask others about theirs.

Chapter 34

Clothes and Fashion

In this chapter, we're going to learn about **Clothes and Fashion** in French. Knowing how to talk about clothing is important because it helps you describe what you're wearing, what you like to wear, and even what's in style. By the end of this chapter, you'll be able to name different types of clothing, describe what people are wearing, and talk about your fashion preferences in French. Let's get started!

Basic Vocabulary for Clothes

Let's start by learning the names of some common clothing items in French:

Shirt - La chemise (lah shuh-meez)

T-shirt - Le tee-shirt (luh tee-shurt)

Pants - Le pantalon (luh pahn-tah-lohn)

Jeans - Le jean (luh zheen)

Skirt - La jupe (lah zhoop)

Dress - La robe (lah rob)

Sweater - Le pull (luh pewl)

Jacket - La veste (lah vest)

Coat - Le manteau (luh mahn-toh)

Shoes - Les chaussures (lay sho-syur)

Sneakers - Les baskets (lay bas-ket)

Hat - Le chapeau (luh shah-poh)

Scarf - L'écharpe (lay-sharp)

These words will help you talk about the different clothing items you wear every day. Now, let's learn how to describe what someone is wearing.

Describing What You're Wearing

If you want to describe what you're wearing, you can use the phrase Je porte... (zhuh port), which means "I'm wearing..." Here's how you can use it:

Je porte une chemise et un pantalon. (zhuh port oon shuh-meez ay uhn pahn-tah-lohn) - I'm wearing a shirt and pants.

Je porte une robe et des chaussures. (zhuh port oon rob ay day sho-syur) - I'm wearing a dress and shoes.

Je porte un pull et un jean. (zhuh port uhn peul ay uhn zheen) - I'm wearing a sweater and jeans.

If you want to describe what someone else is wearing, you can use the phrase Il/Elle porte... (eel/ell port), which means "He/She is wearing..." For example:

Elle porte une jupe et un tee-shirt. (ell port oon zhoop ay uhn tee-shurt) - She's wearing a skirt and a t-shirt.

Il porte un manteau et des baskets. (eel port uhn mahn-toh ay day bas-ket) - He's wearing a coat and sneakers.

These phrases will help you describe your own outfit and ask others about theirs.

Talking About Different Types of Clothing

Clothing can be categorized by what it's for, such as casual wear, formal wear, or sportswear. Here are some phrases to help you talk about different types of clothing in French:

Casual wear - Les vêtements décontractés (lay vet-mahn day-kon-trak-tay)

Formal wear - Les vêtements de cérémonie (lay vet-mahn duh seh-reh-moh-nee)

Sportswear - Les vêtements de sport (lay vet-mahn duh spor)

If you want to say what type of clothing you prefer, you can use the following phrases:

J'aime porter des vêtements décontractés. (zhem por-tay day vet-mahn day-kon-trak-tay) - I like to wear casual clothes.

Je préfère les vêtements de sport. (zhuh pray-fehr lay vet-mahn duh spor) - I prefer sportswear.

Pour les occasions spéciales, je porte des vêtements de cérémonie. (poor layz oh-kah-zyon spay-syal, zhuh port day vet-mahn duh seh-reh-moh-nee) - For special occasions, I wear formal clothes.

These sentences will help you talk about your clothing preferences and the types of clothes you wear for different occasions.

Talking About Fashion Preferences

Fashion, or la mode (lah mod), is about how you like to dress and what styles you prefer. Here's how to talk about fashion in French:

Style - Le style (luh steel)

Trendy - Tendance (tahn-dahnss)

Comfortable - Confortable (kohn-for-tah-bl)

Elegant - Élégant/élégante (ay-lay-gahn/ay-lay-gahnt)

If you want to describe your fashion style, you can say:

Mon style est décontracté et confortable. (mohn steel eh day-kon-trak-tay ay kohn-for-tah-bl) - My style is casual and comfortable.

J'aime porter des vêtements élégants. (zhem por-tay day vet-mahn ay-lay-gahn) - I like to wear elegant clothes.

Je préfère les vêtements tendance. (zhuh pray-fehr lay vet-mahn tahn-dahnss) - I prefer trendy clothes.

If you want to ask someone about their fashion preferences, you can say:

Quel est ton style? (kel eh ton steel) - What's your style?

Aimes-tu porter des vêtements confortables? (em-tew por-tay day vet-mahn kohn-for-tah-bl) - Do you like to wear comfortable clothes?

These phrases will help you talk about fashion and ask others about their preferences.

Talking About Colors and Patterns

When describing clothes, it's also important to talk about colors and patterns. Here are some common colors in French:

Red - Rouge (roozh)

Blue - Bleu (bluh)

Green - Vert/Verte (vehr/vehrt)

Yellow - Jaune (zhohn)

Black - Noir/Noire (nwar/nwahr)

White - Blanc/Blanche (blahn/blahnsh)

Gray - Gris/Grise (gree/greez)

Here are some common patterns in French:

Striped - À rayures (ah ray-yur)

Polka-dotted - À pois (ah pwah)

Checked - À carreaux (ah kah-roh)

Here are some sentences using these words:

Je porte un pull rouge. (zhuh port uhn peul roozh) - I'm wearing a red sweater.

Elle porte une robe bleue à pois. (ell port oon rob bluh ah pwah) - She's wearing a blue polka-dotted dress.

Il porte une chemise à carreaux. (eel port oon shuh-meez ah kah-roh) - He's wearing a checked shirt.

If you want to ask someone about the color or pattern of their clothes, you can say:

De quelle couleur est ta chemise? (duh kel koo-luhr eh tah shuh-meez) - What color is your shirt?

Est-ce que tu aimes les vêtements à rayures? (ess kuh tew em lay vet-mahn ah ray-yur) - Do you like striped clothes?

These phrases will help you describe and ask about the colors and patterns of clothing.

Talking About Shopping for Clothes

If you're shopping for clothes, here are some useful phrases in French:

To shop for clothes - Faire du shopping / Acheter des vêtements (fehr dew shop-ping / ah-shuh-tay day vet-mahn)

Store - Le magasin (luh mah-gah-zan)

Size - La taille (lah tay)

Price - Le prix (luh pree)

To try on - Essayer (eh-say-yay)

Here are some sentences you can use when shopping for clothes:

Je voudrais acheter une nouvelle robe. (zhuh voo-dray ah-shuh-tay oon noo-vel rob) - I would like to buy a new dress.

Quelle est votre taille? (kel eh vo-truh tay) - What's your size?

Puis-je essayer ce pantalon? (pwee-zh eh-say-yay suh pahn-tah-lohn) - Can I try on these pants?

Combien coûte cette veste? (kohm-byen koot set vest) - How much does this jacket cost?

If you want to ask someone if they like shopping for clothes, you can say:

Aimes-tu faire du shopping? (em-tew fehr dew shop-ping) - Do you like shopping?

These phrases will help you talk about buying clothes and ask others about their shopping habits.

Key Points to Remember:

1. **Basic Clothing Vocabulary**: Familiarize yourself with essential clothing items in French, such as la chemise (shirt), le pantalon (pants), and les chaussures (shoes) to discuss everyday wear.

2. **Describing Outfits**: Use phrases like Je porte... (I'm wearing...) and Il/Elle porte... (He/She is wearing...) to describe what you or others are wearing.

3. **Types of Clothing**: Understand how to talk about different types of clothing for various occasions, such as les vêtements décontractés (casual wear) and les vêtements de sport (sportswear).

4. **Fashion Preferences**: Learn to express your style and preferences using terms like tendance (trendy), confortable (comfortable), and élégant/élégante (elegant).

5. **Shopping for Clothes**: Use key phrases for shopping, such as acheter des vêtements (to buy clothes), essayer (to try on), and le prix (price) to navigate clothing stores in French.

Chapter 35

Reflexive Verbs

In this chapter, we're going to learn about **Reflexive Verbs** in French. Reflexive verbs are a special type of verb that show that the action is being done by the subject to itself. This might sound a little tricky at first, but don't worry! By the end of this chapter, you'll understand how reflexive verbs work, and you'll be able to use them in sentences. Let's get started!

What Are Reflexive Verbs?

In English, reflexive verbs are when the subject and the object of the verb are the same. For example, in the sentence "I wash myself," the action of washing is done by the subject (I) to the object (myself), which is the same person. In French, reflexive verbs work in a similar way, but they have a special reflexive pronoun that goes with them.

Reflexive Pronouns

Before we learn how to use reflexive verbs, we need to know the reflexive pronouns in French. These pronouns change depending on who is doing the action. Here they are:

- **Me** (muh) - myself
- **Te** (tuh) - yourself
- **Se** (suh) - himself/herself/itself
- **Nous** (noo) - ourselves
- **Vous** (voo) - yourselves (or formal "yourself")
- **Se** (suh) - themselves

These pronouns come before the verb to show that the subject is doing the action to itself.

How to Conjugate Reflexive Verbs

Let's take a look at how to conjugate reflexive verbs in French. We'll use the verb se laver (suh lah-vay), which means "to wash oneself," as an example. Here's how it works:

- **Je me lave** (zhuh muh lahv) - I wash myself
- **Tu te laves** (tew tuh lahv) - You wash yourself
- **Il/Elle se lave** (eel/ell suh lahv) - He/She washes himself/herself
- **Nous nous lavons** (noo noo lah-vohn) - We wash ourselves
- **Vous vous lavez** (voo voo lah-vay) - You wash yourselves (or You wash yourself - formal)
- **Ils/Elles se lavent** (eel/ell suh lahv) - They wash themselves

Notice how the reflexive pronoun changes with the subject, but the verb laver is conjugated just like a regular -er verb. The reflexive pronoun goes right before the verb in the sentence.

Common Reflexive Verbs

Here are some common reflexive verbs in French that you might use in your daily routine:

- Se réveiller (suh ray-vay-yay) - to wake up
- Se lever (suh luh-vay) - to get up
- Se brosser les dents (suh broh-say lay dahn) - to brush one's teeth
- Se brosser les cheveux (suh broh-say lay shuh-vuh) - to brush one's hair
- Se laver (suh lah-vay) - to wash oneself
- S'habiller (sah-bee-yay) - to get dressed
- Se coucher (suh koo-shay) - to go to bed
- Se reposer (suh ruh-poh-zay) - to rest

These verbs are used frequently when talking about your daily activities. Let's see how to use them in sentences.

Using Reflexive Verbs in Sentences

Let's put these reflexive verbs into action! Here are some examples of sentences using reflexive verbs:

1. Je me réveille à six heures. (zhuh muh ray-vay-yay ah sees uhr) - I wake up at six o'clock.

2. Tu te brosses les dents après le petit déjeuner. (tew tuh brohss lay dahn ah-pray luh puh-tee day-zhuh-nay) - You brush your teeth after breakfast.

3. Elle se lave le visage tous les matins. (ell suh lahv luh vee-zahzh too lay mah-tan) - She washes her face every morning.

4. Nous nous habillons avant de sortir. (noo noo sah-bee-yon ah-vahn duh sor-teer) - We get dressed before going out.

5. Ils se reposent après l'école. (eel suh ruh-pohz ah-pray lay-kohl) - They rest after school.

In each of these sentences, the reflexive pronoun matches the subject of the verb and shows that the action is being done to oneself.

Negative Form of Reflexive Verbs

Just like with regular verbs, you can make reflexive verbs negative by putting ne...pas around the reflexive pronoun and the verb. Here's how it works:

Je ne me lève pas tôt le week-end. (zhuh nuh muh lev pah toh luh week-end) - I don't get up early on the weekend.

Elle ne se maquille pas souvent. (ell nuh suh mah-keey pah soo-vahn) - She doesn't put on makeup often.

In these examples, ne comes before the reflexive pronoun, and pas comes after the verb. This makes the sentence negative.

Reflexive Verbs in the Past Tense

When using reflexive verbs in the past tense (passé composé), you need to use the auxiliary verb être (eh-tr) and make sure the past participle agrees with the subject. Here's how it works with the verb se lever (suh luh-vay):

- **Je me suis levé(e)** (zhuh muh swee luh-vay) - I got up
- **Tu t'es levé(e)** (tew teh luh-vay) - You got up
- **Il/Elle s'est levé(e)** (eel/ell seh luh-vay) - He/She got up

- **Nous nous sommes levé(e)s** (noo noo sohm luh-vay) - We got up

- **Vous vous êtes levé(e)(s)** (voo voo zet luh-vay) - You got up

- **Ils/Elles se sont levé(e)(s)** (eel/ell suh sohn luh-vay) - They got up

Notice that the past participle levé agrees with the subject in gender and number. For example, if a girl says, "I got up," she would say, Je me suis levée (zhuh muh swee luh-vay), with an extra "e" at the end. If a group of boys says, "We got up," they would say, Nous nous sommes levés (noo noo sohm luh-vay), with an "s" at the end.

Using Reflexive Verbs to Talk About Daily Routines

Reflexive verbs are very useful when talking about your daily routine. Here's an example of a daily routine using reflexive verbs:

Je me réveille à 7 heures. Ensuite, je me lève et je me brosse les dents. Après ça, je m'habille et je me prépare pour l'école. Le soir, je me repose un peu avant de faire mes devoirs. Puis , je me douche et je me couche vers 10 heures.

(Translation: I wake up at 7 o'clock. Then, I get up and brush my teeth. After that, I get dressed and get ready for school. In the evening, I rest a bit before doing my homework. Then, I take a shower and go to bed around 10 o'clock.)

In this example, you can see how reflexive verbs are used to describe everyday actions.

Key Points to Remember:

1. **Understanding Reflexive Verbs**: Reflexive verbs show that the action is done by the subject to itself. They use reflexive pronouns like me, te, se, and nous to indicate this.

2. **Conjugation of Reflexive Verbs**: Reflexive verbs are conjugated with the appropriate reflexive pronoun before the verb. For example, se laver becomes je me lave (I wash myself).

3. **Common Reflexive Verbs**: Some common reflexive verbs include se réveiller (to wake up), se laver (to wash oneself), and s'habiller (to get dressed).

4. **Negative Form**: To make a reflexive verb negative, place ne...pas around the reflexive pronoun and the verb, e.g., je ne me lève pas (I don't get up).

5. **Past Tense Usage**: In the past tense, reflexive verbs use être as the auxiliary verb, and the past participle agrees in gender and number with the subject, e.g., je me suis levé(e) (I got up).

Chapter 36

Past Tense: Passé Composé

In this chapter, we're going to learn about the **Past Tense: Passé Composé** in French. The passé composé is used to talk about actions that happened in the past. It's one of the most common past tenses in French, so it's important to understand how to form it and when to use it. By the end of this chapter, you'll be able to create sentences in the passé composé and talk about things that happened in the past. Let's get started!

What Is the Passé Composé?

The passé composé is used to describe actions that are completed and happened at a specific time in the past. In English, it's similar to using the simple past tense, like saying "I ate" or "They went." In French, the passé composé is made up of two parts: the auxiliary verb (also called the helping verb) and the past participle.

Auxiliary Verbs: Avoir and Être

To form the passé composé, you first need to know the auxiliary verbs. There are two auxiliary verbs in French that you'll use: avoir (ah-vwahr), which means "to have," and être (eh-tr), which means "to be." Most verbs use avoir as the auxiliary verb, but some special verbs use être. Let's start with avoir.

Here's how avoir is conjugated:

- **J'ai** (zhay) - I have
- **Tu as** (tew ah) - You have
- **Il/Elle a** (eel/ell ah) - He/She has
- **Nous avons** (noo zah-vohn) - We have
- **Vous avez** (voo zah-vay) - You have
- **Ils/Elles ont** (eel/ell zohn) - They have

And here's how être is conjugated:

- **Je suis** (zhuh swee) - I am

- **Tu es** (tew eh) - You are

- **Il/Elle est** (eel/ell eh) - He/She is

- **Nous sommes** (noo sohm) - We are

- **Vous êtes** (voo zet) - You are

- **Ils/Elles sont** (eel/ell sohn) - They are

Past Participles

After choosing the correct auxiliary verb, the next step is to add the past participle of the main verb. The past participle is a special form of the verb that shows the action has been completed. Here's how to form the past participle for regular verbs:

- **-er verbs:** Replace -er with -é. For example, parler (par-lay) becomes parlé (par-lay), which means "spoken."

- **-ir verbs:** Replace -ir with -i. For example, finir (fee-neer) becomes fini (fee-nee), which means "finished."

- **-re verbs:** Replace -re with -u. For example, vendre (vahn-druh) becomes vendu (vahn-dew), which means "sold."

Some verbs have irregular past participles, which you'll need to memorize. For example, avoir becomes eu (ew), être becomes été (ay-tay), and faire (to do/make) becomes fait (feh).

Forming the Passé Composé with Avoir

Now let's see how to form the passé composé with the auxiliary verb avoir. We'll use the verb parler (to speak) as an example:

- **J'ai parlé** (zhay par-lay) - I spoke / I have spoken

- **Tu as parlé** (tew ah par-lay) - You spoke / You have spoken

- **Il/Elle a parlé** (eel/ell ah par-lay) - He/She spoke / He/She has spoken

- **Nous avons parlé** (noo zah-vohn par-lay) - We spoke / We have spoken

- **Vous avez parlé** (voo zah-vay par-lay) - You spoke / You have spoken
- **Ils/Elles ont parlé** (eel/ell zohn par-lay) - They spoke / They have spoken

Notice how the past participle parlé stays the same no matter who the subject is. This is true for all verbs that use avoir as the auxiliary verb.

Forming the Passé Composé with Être

Some verbs use être as the auxiliary verb in the passé composé. These are often verbs of motion, like aller (to go), venir (to come), arriver (to arrive), and partir (to leave). Here's how to form the passé composé with être using the verb aller (to go) as an example:

- **Je suis allé(e)** (zhuh swee ah-lay) - I went / I have gone
- **Tu es allé(e)** (tew eh ah-lay) - You went / You have gone
- **Il/Elle est allé(e)** (eel/ell eh ah-lay) - He/She went / He/She has gone
- **Nous sommes allé(e)s** (noo sohm ah-lay) - We went / We have gone
- **Vous êtes allé(e)(s)** (voo zet ah-lay) - You went / You have gone
- **Ils/Elles sont allé(e)s** (eel/ell sohn ah-lay) - They went / They have gone

When using être as the auxiliary verb, the past participle must agree with the subject in gender and number. This means you add an "e" if the subject is feminine and an "s" if the subject is plural. For example, if a girl says "I went," she would say Je suis allée (zhuh swee ah-lay), with an extra "e" at the end. If a group of boys says "We went," they would say Nous sommes allés (noo sohm ah-lay), with an "s" at the end.

Verbs That Use Être in the Passé Composé

Here's a list of some common verbs that use être as the auxiliary verb in the passé composé. A good way to remember them is with the acronym DR & MRS VANDERTRAMP:

- **D** - Devenir (to become) - devenu (duh-vuh-new)
- **R** - Revenir (to come back) - revenu (ruh-vuh-new)
- **M** - Monter (to go up) - monté (mohn-tay)
- **R** - Rentrer (to return) - rentré (rahn-tray)
- **S** - Sortir (to go out) - sorti (sor-tee)

- **V** - Venir (to come) - venu (vuh-new)
- **A** - Arriver (to arrive) - arrivé (ah-ree-vay)
- **N** - Naître (to be born) - né (nay)
- **D** - Descendre (to go down) - descendu (day-sahn-dew)
- **E** - Entrer (to enter) - entré (ahn-tray)
- **R** - Retourner (to return) - retourné (ruh-toor-nay)
- **T** - Tomber (to fall) - tombé (tohm-bay)
- **R** - Rester (to stay) - resté (res-tay)
- **A** - Aller (to go) - allé (ah-lay)
- **M** - Mourir (to die) - mort (mor)
- **P** - Partir (to leave) - parti (par-tee)

These verbs are exceptions to the rule of using avoir as the auxiliary verb. Remember to make the past participle agree with the subject in gender and number when using être.

Using the Passé Composé in Sentences

Let's see how to use the passé composé in sentences. Here are some examples:

J'ai mangé une pizza hier soir. (zhay mahn-zhay oon peet-sah yehr swahr) - I ate a pizza last night.

Elle est allée au cinéma avec ses amis. (ell eh tah-lay oh see-nay-mah ah-vek sayz ah-mee) - She went to the movies with her friends.

Nous avons fini nos devoirs avant le dîner. (noo zah-vohn fee-nee noh duh-vwahr ah-vahn luh dee-nay) - We finished our homework before dinner.

Ils sont venus à la fête samedi dernier. (eel sohn vuh-new ah lah fet sahm-dee dehr-nyay) - They came to the party last Saturday.

In each of these sentences, the passé composé is used to describe an action that was completed in the past.

Negative Form of the Passé Composé

You can also make the passé composé negative by putting ne...pas around the auxiliary verb. Here's how it works:

Je n'ai pas regardé la télévision hier. (zhuh nay pah ruh-gar-day lah tay-lay-vee-zyon yehr) - I didn't watch TV yesterday.

Elle n'est pas venue à l'école aujourd'hui. (ell neh pah vuh-new ah lay-kohl oh-zhoor-dwee) - She didn't come to school today.

Notice that ne comes before the auxiliary verb and pas comes after it, making the sentence negative.

Key Points to Remember:

- **Formation of Passé Composé:** The passé composé is formed using an auxiliary verb (either "avoir" or "être") followed by the past participle of the main verb.

- **Auxiliary Verbs:** Most verbs use "avoir" as the auxiliary verb, but certain verbs, particularly those indicating motion or change of state, use "être."

- **Past Participle Agreement:** When using "être" as the auxiliary verb, the past participle must agree with the subject in gender and number.

- **Common Verbs with Être:** Remember the verbs that use "être" in the passé composé with the acronym DR & MRS VANDERTRAMP.

- **Negative Form:** To make a sentence in the passé composé negative, place "ne...pas" around the auxiliary verb.

Chapter 37

Past Tense: Imparfait

In this chapter, we're going to learn about the **Past Tense: Imparfait** in French. The imparfait is another way to talk about the past, but it's used differently than the passé composé. While the passé composé is used for specific, completed actions in the past, the imparfait is used to describe ongoing or repeated actions, habits, or background information. By the end of this chapter, you'll be able to form the imparfait and use it to describe what things were like in the past. Let's get started!

What Is the Imparfait?

The imparfait is used to talk about things that were happening continuously or repeatedly in the past. It's similar to the English phrases "I was doing" or "I used to do." The imparfait can also be used to set the scene or describe how things were in the past. For example, you might use the imparfait to say, "When I was little, I used to play outside every day," or "It was raining yesterday."

How to Form the Imparfait

Forming the imparfait is easier than you might think! Here's a simple formula to follow:

   1. Take the **nous** form of the verb in the present tense.

   2. Remove the **-ons** ending.

   3. Add the imparfait endings.

Let's take the verb parler (to speak) as an example:

   1. Find the **nous** form: nous parlons (noo par-lon) - we speak.

   2. Remove the **-ons** ending: parl-

   3. Add the imparfait endings:

- **Je parlais** (zhuh par-lay) - I was speaking / I used to speak

- **Tu parlais** (tew par-lay) - You were speaking / You used to speak

- **Il/Elle parlait** (eel/ell par-lay) - He/She was speaking / He/She used to speak

- **Nous parlions** (noo par-lyon) - We were speaking / We used to speak

- **Vous parliez** (voo par-lyay) - You were speaking / You used to speak

- **Ils/Elles parlaient** (eel/ell par-lay) - They were speaking / They used to speak

Notice that the endings are the same for all verbs in the imparfait, regardless of whether the verb ends in -er, -ir, or -re. The endings are:

- **-ais** (ay)

- **-ais** (ay)

- **-ait** (ay)

- **-ions** (yon)

- **-iez** (yay)

- **-aient** (ay)

Using the Imparfait to Describe Ongoing Actions

One of the main uses of the imparfait is to describe actions that were ongoing in the past. These are actions that don't have a clear beginning or end and were happening over a period of time. Here are some examples:

Je lisais un livre quand il a commencé à pleuvoir. (zhuh lee-zay uhn leevr kawn eel ah koh-mahn-say ah pleuh-vwahr) - I was reading a book when it started to rain.

Ils regardaient la télévision pendant que je faisais mes devoirs. (eel ruh-gar-day lah tay-lay-vee-zyon pahn-dahn kuh zhuh feh-zay may duh-vwahr) - They were watching TV while I was doing my homework.

Nous jouions dehors chaque après-midi. (noo zhwee-yon duh-or shak ah-pray-mee-dee) - We used to play outside every afternoon.

In these sentences, the imparfait is used to describe what was happening in the background or what was happening continuously over time.

Using the Imparfait to Describe Habits and Repeated Actions

The imparfait is also used to describe habits or actions that were repeated in the past. These are things that you used to do regularly. Here are some examples:

Quand j'étais petit(e), je jouais avec mes amis tous les jours. (kawn zhuh-tay puh-tee, zhuh zhway ah-vek mayz ah-mee too lay zhoor) - When I was little, I used to play with my friends every day.

Nous allions à la plage chaque été. (noo zah-lyon ah lah plahzh shak ay-tay) - We used to go to the beach every summer.

Elle faisait du vélo tous les dimanches. (ell feh-zay dew vay-loh too lay dee-mahnsh) - She used to ride her bike every Sunday.

In these sentences, the imparfait is used to describe actions that were done regularly or habitually in the past.

Using the Imparfait to Set the Scene or Describe Background Information

Another use of the imparfait is to set the scene or provide background information in a story. This includes describing the weather, how things looked, or what was going on in the background. Here are some examples:

Il faisait beau et le soleil brillait. (eel fuh-zay boh ay luh soh-lay bree-yay) - It was a beautiful day, and the sun was shining.

La maison était grande et vieille. (lah may-zon eh-tay grahnd ay vye-yay) - The house was big and old.

Les enfants jouaient dans le jardin pendant que les adultes discutaient. (layz ahn-fahn zhway-eh dahn luh zhar-dan pahn-dahn kuh layz ah-doolt dees-kyoo-tay) - The children were playing in the garden while the adults were chatting.

In these sentences, the imparfait is used to describe the setting and give more details about what was happening around the main action.

Irregular Verbs in the Imparfait

Most verbs in French follow the regular rules for forming the imparfait, but there are a few irregular verbs that you need to watch out for. The most common irregular verb in the imparfait is être (to be). Here's how it's conjugated:

- **J'étais** (zhuh-tay) - I was

- **Tu étais** (tew eh-tay) - You were

- **Il/Elle était** (eel/ell eh-tay) - He/She was

- **Nous étions** (noo zay-tyon) - We were

- **Vous étiez** (voo zay-tyay) - You were

- **Ils/Elles étaient** (eel/ell eh-tay) - They were

Since être is irregular, it doesn't follow the normal rule of dropping the -ons from the nous form. Instead, you'll need to memorize its special conjugation in the imparfait.

Using the Imparfait with the Passé Composé

Sometimes, the imparfait and the passé composé are used together in the same sentence. The imparfait is used to describe what was happening or what things were like in the background, while the passé composé is used for specific actions that interrupt or occur during that ongoing action. Here's how they work together:

Je lisais un livre quand le téléphone a sonné. (zhuh lee-zay uhn leevr kawn luh tay-lay-fohn ah soh-nay) - I was reading a book when the phone rang.

Ils regardaient la télé quand ils ont entendu un bruit étrange. (eel ruh-gar-day lah tay-lay kawn eelz ohn ahn-tahn-dew uhn br wee ay-trahnzh) - They were watching TV when they heard a strange noise.

Nous marchions dans la rue quand il a commencé à pleuvoir. (noo mar-shyon dahn lah roo kawn eel ah koh-mahn-say ah pleuh-vwahr) - We were walking down the street when it started to rain.

In these sentences, the imparfait sets the scene and describes what was happening when something specific occurred, which is expressed in the passé composé.

Negative Form of the Imparfait

Just like with other tenses, you can make the imparfait negative by putting ne...pas around the verb. Here's how it works:

Je ne jouais pas dehors hier. (zhuh nuh zhway pah duh-or yehr) - I wasn't playing outside yesterday.

Ils n'étudiaient pas pour l'examen. (eelz nay-too-dyay pah poor lek-sah-mahn) - They weren't studying for the exam.

Notice that ne comes before the verb and pas comes after it, making the sentence negative.

Key Points to Remember:

1. **Formation of Imparfait:** The imparfait is formed by taking the "nous" form of a verb in the present tense, removing the "-ons" ending, and adding the imparfait endings (-ais, -ais, -ait, -ions, -iez, -aient).

2. **Uses of Imparfait:** The imparfait is used to describe ongoing or repeated actions in the past, such as habits, background information, or setting the scene.

3. **Irregular Verbs:** While most verbs follow regular conjugation patterns in the imparfait, "être" is an important irregular verb to remember, with its unique conjugation.

4. **Combining with Passé Composé:** The imparfait is often used alongside the passé composé in the same sentence to describe ongoing actions that were interrupted by specific events.

5. **Negative Form:** To make a verb in the imparfait negative, place "ne...pas" around the verb, just as in other tenses.

Chapter 38

Future Tense

In this chapter, we're going to learn about the **Future Tense** in French. The future tense is used to talk about actions that will happen or things that will take place in the future. It's like saying "I will go" or "They will eat" in English. By the end of this chapter, you'll be able to form the future tense in French and use it to talk about your plans and predictions. Let's get started!

What Is the Future Tense?

The future tense in French, known as le futur simple (luh fyoo-toor san-pl), is used to describe actions that will happen in the future. This tense is straightforward because you only need to know the infinitive form of the verb and a set of endings that you'll add to it. Let's see how it works.

How to Form the Future Tense

Forming the future tense in French is simple. You follow these steps:

1. Take the infinitive form of the verb (the base form you find in the dictionary).

2. Add the future tense endings to the infinitive.

Here are the future tense endings:

- **-ai** (ay)
- **-as** (ah)
- **-a** (ah)
- **-ons** (ohn)
- **-ez** (ay)
- **-ont** (ohn)

Let's use the verb parler (to speak) as an example:

- **Je parlerai** (zhuh par-luh-ray) - I will speak
- **Tu parleras** (tew par-luh-rah) - You will speak
- **Il/Elle parlera** (eel/ell par-luh-rah) - He/She will speak
- **Nous parlerons** (noo par-luh-rohn) - We will speak
- **Vous parlerez** (voo par-luh-ray) - You will speak
- **Ils/Elles parleront** (eel/ell par-luh-rohn) - They will speak

Notice that the endings are the same for all regular verbs, and the infinitive form of the verb doesn't change. This makes forming the future tense very easy.

Future Tense for Regular Verbs

Most verbs in French are regular, meaning they follow the same pattern when forming the future tense. Here's how to form the future tense for each type of regular verb:

-er verbs: Simply add the future tense endings to the infinitive.

Example with aimer (to like/love):

- **J'aimerai** (zhay-muh-ray) - I will like
- **Tu aimeras** (tew ay-muh-rah) - You will like
- **Il/Elle aimera** (eel/ell ay-muh-rah) - He/She will like
- **Nous aimerons** (noo ay-muh-rohn) - We will like
- **Vous aimerez** (voo ay-muh-ray) - You will like
- **Ils/Elles aimeront** (eel/ell ay-muh-rohn) - They will like

-ir verbs: Add the future tense endings directly to the infinitive.

Example with finir (to finish):

- **Je finirai** (zhuh fee-nee-ray) - I will finish
- **Tu finiras** (tew fee-nee-rah) - You will finish
- **Il/Elle finira** (eel/ell fee-nee-rah) - He/She will finish

- **Nous finirons** (noo fee-nee-rohn) - We will finish

- **Vous finirez** (voo fee-nee-ray) - You will finish

- **Ils/Elles finiront** (eel/ell fee-nee-rohn) - They will finish

-re verbs: For verbs ending in -re, drop the final -e from the infinitive before adding the future tense endings.

Example with vendre (to sell):

- **Je vendrai** (zhuh vahn-dray) - I will sell

- **Tu vendras** (tew vahn-drah) - You will sell

- **Il/Elle vendra** (eel/ell vahn-drah) - He/She will sell

- **Nous vendrons** (noo vahn-drohn) - We will sell

- **Vous vendrez** (voo vahn-dray) - You will sell

- **Ils/Elles vendront** (eel/ell vahn-drohn) - They will sell

Future Tense for Irregular Verbs

Some verbs in French are irregular in the future tense, meaning they don't follow the regular pattern. Instead, they have a special stem that you need to memorize. The good news is that once you know the stem, you just add the regular future tense endings. Here are some common irregular verbs in the future tense:

- **Être** (to be) - ser- becomes je serai (zhuh suh-ray) - I will be

- **Avoir** (to have) - aur- becomes j'aurai (zhuh-ray) - I will have

- **Aller** (to go) - ir- becomes j'irai (zhee-ray) - I will go

- **Faire** (to do/make) - fer- becomes je ferai (zhuh fuh-ray) - I will do/make

- **Venir** (to come) - viendr- becomes je viendrai (zhuh vyan-dray) - I will come

- **Voir** (to see) - verr- becomes je verrai (zhuh vehr-ray) - I will see

For example, let's look at the verb être (to be):

- **Je serai** (zhuh suh-ray) - I will be

- **Tu seras** (tew suh-rah) - You will be
- **Il/Elle sera** (eel/ell suh-rah) - He/She will be
- **Nous serons** (noo suh-rohn) - We will be
- **Vous serez** (voo suh-ray) - You will be
- **Ils/Elles seront** (eel/ell suh-rohn) - They will be

Even though être is irregular, you can see that the endings are the same as for regular verbs. The only difference is the stem, which changes to ser-.

Using the Future Tense in Sentences

Now that you know how to form the future tense, let's see how to use it in sentences. Here are some examples:

Je voyagerai en France l'année prochaine. (zhuh vwa-yah-zhuh-ray ahn frahn ss lah-nay pro-shen) - I will travel to France next year.

Nous mangerons au restaurant ce soir. (noo mahn-zhuh-rohn oh res-toh-rahn suh swahr) - We will eat at the restaurant tonight.

Ils finiront leurs devoirs après l'école. (eel fee-nee-rohn luhr duh-vwahr ah-pray lay-kohl) - They will finish their homework after school.

Elle ira à la piscine demain. (ell eer-ah ah lah pee-seen duh-mahn) - She will go to the pool tomorrow.

In each of these sentences, the future tense is used to talk about actions that will happen at a later time.

Using the Future Tense to Make Predictions

The future tense is often used to make predictions about what will happen. Here are some examples:

Il fera beau demain. (eel fuh-rah boh duh-mahn) - It will be nice weather tomorrow.

Tu réussiras ton examen. (tew ray-oo-see-rah ton eg-zah-mahn) - You will pass your exam.

Nous gagnerons le match. (noo gah-nye-rohn luh match) - We will win the game.

In these sentences, the future tense is used to predict what will happen in the future.

Using the Future Tense to Talk About Future Plans

You can also use the future tense to talk about your plans for the future. Here's how:

Je travaillerai cet été. (zhuh tra-vah-yuh-ray set ay-tay) - I will work this summer.

Nous visiterons Paris en août. (noo vee-zee-toh-rohn pah-ree ahn oot) - We will visit Paris in August.

Ils achèteront une nouvelle maison l'année prochaine. (eelz ah-sheh-tuh-rohn oon noo-vel may-zon lah-nay pro-shen) - They will buy a new house next year.

In these examples, the future tense is used to express plans and intentions.

Negative Form of the Future Tense

Just like with other tenses, you can make the future tense negative by putting ne...pas around the verb. Here's how it works:

Je ne voyagerai pas cet été. (zhuh nuh vwa-yah-zhuh-ray pah set ay-tay) - I will not travel this summer.

Ils ne finiront pas leurs devoirs ce soir. (eelz nuh fee-nee-rohn pah luhr duh-vwahr suh swahr) - They will not finish their homework tonight.

Notice that ne comes before the verb and pas comes after it, making the sentence negative.

Key Points to Remember:

1. **Formation of Future Tense:** The future tense in French is formed by adding specific endings (-ai, -as, -a, -ons, -ez, -ont) to the infinitive form of regular verbs.

2. **Regular Verbs:** Regular -er, -ir, and -re verbs follow the same pattern in the future tense, with -re verbs requiring the removal of the final -e before adding the endings.

3. **Irregular Verbs:** Some verbs have irregular stems in the future tense, like "être" (ser-), "avoir" (aur-), and "aller" (ir-), but they still use the regular future tense endings.

4. **Using the Future Tense:** The future tense is used to describe actions that will happen, make predictions, or talk about future plans.

5. **Negative Form:** To make the future tense negative, place "ne...pas" around the verb, just as in other tenses.

Chapter 39

Conditional Mood

In this chapter, we're going to learn about the **Conditional Mood** in French. The conditional mood is used to talk about what would happen if certain conditions were met. It's like saying "I would go" or "They would eat" in English. By the end of this chapter, you'll be able to form the conditional mood in French and use it to talk about possibilities, hypothetical situations, and polite requests. Let's get started!

What Is the Conditional Mood?

The conditional mood, or le conditionnel (luh kohn-dee-syo-nel), is used to express what would happen if a certain condition were met. It's often used to talk about things that are possible or hypothetical. For example, you might say, "I would travel if I had the money," or "She would go to the party if she were invited." The conditional mood is also used to make polite requests or suggestions, like saying, "Could you help me?" or "I would like a coffee."

How to Form the Conditional Mood

Forming the conditional mood in French is simple if you already know how to form the future tense. Here's the formula:

1. Take the infinitive form of the verb (the base form you find in the dictionary).

2. Add the conditional endings, which are the same as the imperfect endings.

Here are the conditional endings:

- **-ais** (ay)

- **-ais** (ay)

- **-ait** (ay)

- **-ions** (yon)

- **-iez** (yay)
- **-aient** (ay)

Let's use the verb parler (to speak) as an example:

- **Je parlerais** (zhuh par-luh-ray) - I would speak
- **Tu parlerais** (tew par-luh-ray) - You would speak
- **Il/Elle parlerait** (eel/ell par-luh-ray) - He/She would speak
- **Nous parlerions** (noo par-lyon) - We would speak
- **Vous parleriez** (voo par-lyay) - You would speak
- **Ils/Elles parleraient** (eel/ell par-luh-ray) - They would speak

Notice that the endings are the same as the imperfect tense, and the infinitive form of the verb doesn't change, just like in the future tense.

Conditional Mood for Regular Verbs

Most verbs in French are regular, meaning they follow the same pattern when forming the conditional mood. Here's how to form the conditional mood for each type of regular verb:

-er verbs: Simply add the conditional endings to the infinitive.

Example with aimer (to like/love):

- **J'aimerais** (zhay-muh-ray) - I would like
- **Tu aimerais** (tew ay-muh-ray) - You would like
- **Il/Elle aimerait** (eel/ell ay-muh-ray) - He/She would like
- **Nous aimerions** (noo ay-muh-ryon) - We would like
- **Vous aimeriez** (voo ay-muh-ryay) - You would like
- **Ils/Elles aimeraient** (eel/ell ay-muh-ray) - They would like

-ir verbs: Add the conditional endings directly to the infinitive.

Example with finir (to finish):

- **Je finirais** (zhuh fee-nee-ray) - I would finish

- **Tu finirais** (tew fee-nee-ray) - You would finish
- **Il/Elle finirait** (eel/ell fee-nee-ray) - He/She would finish
- **Nous finirions** (noo fee-nee-ryon) - We would finish
- **Vous finiriez** (voo fee-nee-ryay) - You would finish
- **Ils/Elles finiraient** (eel/ell fee-nee-ray) - They would finish

-re verbs: For verbs ending in -re, drop the final -e from the infinitive before adding the conditional endings.

Example with vendre (to sell):

- **Je vendrais** (zhuh vahn-dray) - I would sell
- **Tu vendrais** (tew vahn-dray) - You would sell
- **Il/Elle vendrait** (eel/ell vahn-dray) - He/She would sell
- **Nous vendrions** (noo vahn-dree-yon) - We would sell
- **Vous vendriez** (voo vahn-dree-yay) - You would sell
- **Ils/Elles vendraient** (eel/ell vahn-dray) - They would sell

Conditional Mood for Irregular Verbs

Just like with the future tense, some verbs in French are irregular in the conditional mood. These verbs have a special stem that you need to memorize. Once you know the stem, you add the regular conditional endings. Here are some common irregular verbs in the conditional mood:

- **Être** (to be) - ser- becomes je serais (zhuh suh-ray) - I would be
- **Avoir** (to have) - aur- becomes j'aurais (zhuh-ray) - I would have
- **Aller** (to go) - ir- becomes j'irais (zhee-ray) - I would go
- **Faire** (to do/make) - fer- becomes je ferais (zhuh fuh-ray) - I would do/make
- **Venir** (to come) - viendr- becomes je viendrais (zhuh vyan-dray) - I would come
- **Voir** (to see) - verr- becomes je verrais (zhuh vehr-ray) - I would see

For example, let's look at the verb être (to be):

- **Je serais** (zhuh suh-ray) - I would be
- **Tu serais** (tew suh-ray) - You would be
- **Il/Elle serait** (eel/ell suh-ray) - He/She would be
- **Nous serions** (noo suh-ryon) - We would be
- **Vous seriez** (voo suh-ryay) - You would be
- **Ils/Elles seraient** (eel/ell suh-ray) - They would be

Even though être is irregular, you can see that the endings are the same as for regular verbs. The only difference is the stem, which changes to ser-.

Using the Conditional Mood in Sentences

Now that you know how to form the conditional mood, let's see how to use it in sentences. Here are some examples:

Je voyagerais si j'avais assez d'argent. (zhuh vwa-yah-zhuh-ray see zhah-vay ah-say dar-zhahn) - I would travel if I had enough money.

Nous mangerions au restaurant si nous avions le temps. (noo mahn-zhuh-ryon oh res-toh-rahn see noo zah-vyon luh tan) - We would eat at the restaurant if we had time.

Ils finiraient leurs devoirs plus tôt s'ils pouvaient. (eel fee-nee-ray luhr duh-vwahr ploo toh seel poo-vay) - They would finish their homework earlier if they could.

Elle irait à la plage si elle n'était pas malade. (ell eer-ray ah lah plahzh see ell nay-tay pah mah-lahd) - She would go to the beach if she weren't sick.

In each of these sentences, the conditional mood is used to talk about what would happen under certain conditions.

Using the Conditional Mood for Polite Requests

The conditional mood is also used to make polite requests or suggestions. Here's how:

Pourriez-vous m'aider? (poo-ree-ay voo may-day) - Could you help me?

Je voudrais un café, s'il vous plaît. (zhuh voo-dray uhn kah-fay, seel voo pleh) - I would like a coffee, please.

Nous aimerions réserver une table. (noo zay-muh-ryon ray-zay-vay oon tah-bluh) - We would like to reserve a table.

In these examples, the conditional mood is used to make requests or express desires in a polite way.

Using the Conditional Mood to Talk About Possibilities

The conditional mood is often used to talk about things that are possible but not certain. Here are some examples:

Il pourrait neiger demain. (eel poo-ray nay-zhay duh-mahn) - It could snow tomorrow.

Elle achèterait cette robe si elle avait assez d'argent. (ell ah-sheh-tuh-ray set rob see ell ah-vay ah-say dar-zhahn) - She would buy this dress if she had enough money.

Nous viendrions à ta fête, mais nous sommes occupés. (noo vyan-dree-yon ah tah fet, meh noo sohmz oh-koo-pay) - We would come to your party, but we're busy.

In these sentences, the conditional mood is used to talk about possibilities or things that might happen under certain circumstances.

Negative Form of the Conditional Mood

Just like with other tenses, you can make the conditional mood negative by putting ne...pas around the verb. Here's how it works:

Je ne voyagerais pas cet été. (zhuh nuh vwa-yah-zhuh-ray pah set ay-tay) - I would not travel this summer.

Ils ne finiraient pas leurs devoirs ce soir. (eelz nuh fee-nee-ray pah luhr duh-vwahr suh swahr) - They would not finish their homework tonight.

Notice that ne comes before the verb and pas comes after it, making the sentence negative.

Key Points to Remember:

1. **Formation of Conditional Mood:** The conditional mood in French is formed by adding the same endings as the imperfect tense (-ais, -ais, -ait, -ions, -iez, -aient) to the infinitive form of the verb.

2. **Regular Verbs:** For regular -er, -ir, and -re verbs, the conditional is formed by simply adding the conditional endings to the infinitive, with -re verbs requiring the removal of the final -e.

3. **Irregular Verbs:** Some verbs have irregular stems in the conditional mood, like "être" (ser-), "avoir" (aur-), and "aller" (ir-), but they still use the regular conditional endings.

4. **Usage of Conditional Mood:** The conditional mood is used to talk about what would happen under certain conditions, make polite requests, and discuss possibilities.

5. **Negative Form:** To make the conditional mood negative, place "ne...pas" around the verb, just as in other tenses.

Chapter 40

Subjunctive Mood

In this chapter, we're going to learn about the **Subjunctive Mood** in French. The subjunctive mood is used to express doubts, wishes, emotions, possibilities, and other situations that are not certain. While it might seem tricky at first, understanding the subjunctive will help you express yourself more fully in French. By the end of this chapter, you'll know when and how to use the subjunctive mood. Let's get started!

What Is the Subjunctive Mood?

The subjunctive mood, or le subjonctif (luh soob-zhon-teef), is used to express things that are not certain or that are influenced by emotions, desires, doubts, or opinions. Unlike the indicative mood, which is used to state facts, the subjunctive mood is used when there is some degree of uncertainty or subjectivity. For example, you might use the subjunctive to say, "I want you to come," or "It's important that she be on time."

How to Form the Subjunctive Mood

Forming the subjunctive mood in French involves taking the stem of the verb and adding a specific set of endings. Here's the general process:

1. Take the **ils/elles** form of the verb in the present tense.

2. Remove the **-ent** ending to get the stem.

3. Add the subjunctive endings.

Here are the subjunctive endings:

- **-e** (uh)

- **-es** (uh)

- **-e** (uh)

- **-ions** (yon)

- **-iez** (yay)

- **-ent** (uh)

Let's use the verb parler (to speak) as an example:

- **Que je parle** (kuh zhuh parl) - That I speak

- **Que tu parles** (kuh tew parl) - That you speak

- **Qu'il/elle parle** (keel/ell parl) - That he/she speaks

- **Que nous parlions** (kuh noo parl-yon) - That we speak

- **Que vous parliez** (kuh voo parl-yay) - That you speak

- **Qu'ils/elles parlent** (keel/ell parl) - That they speak

Notice that the subjunctive endings are very similar to the present tense endings, but with a slight difference in the **nous** and **vous** forms.

When to Use the Subjunctive Mood

Knowing when to use the subjunctive can be challenging, but there are some common situations where it's required. Here are the main scenarios where you'll need the subjunctive mood:

1. Expressing Wishes or Desires

The subjunctive is often used after verbs that express a wish or desire. Here are some examples:

Je veux que tu fasses tes devoirs. (zhuh vuh kuh tew fass tay duh-vwahr) - I want you to do your homework.

Elle souhaite que nous soyons à l'heure. (ell soo-et kuh noo swah-yon ah luhr) - She wishes that we be on time.

Ils préfèrent que vous veniez demain. (eel pray-fehr kuh voo vuh-nyee duh-mahn) - They prefer that you come tomorrow.

In these sentences, the subjunctive is used after verbs like vouloir (to want), souhaiter (to wish), and préférer (to prefer) to express a desire.

2. Expressing Doubts or Uncertainty

The subjunctive is also used to express doubts or uncertainty. Here are some examples:

Je doute qu'il vienne. (zhuh doot keel vyen) - I doubt that he will come.

Il est possible qu'elle soit malade. (eel eh poh-see-bl kel swah mah-lahd) - It's possible that she is sick.

Nous ne pensons pas qu'ils aient raison. (noo nuh pahn-son pah keelz ay ray-zon) - We don't think that they are right.

In these sentences, the subjunctive is used after phrases that express doubt or uncertainty, like douter (to doubt) and il est possible que (it is possible that).

3. Expressing Emotions or Feelings

When expressing emotions or feelings about something, the subjunctive is often used. Here are some examples:

Je suis content(e) que tu sois ici. (zhuh swee kohn-tahn/te kuh tew swah ee-see) - I am happy that you are here.

Elle est triste qu'il parte. (ell eh treest keel part) - She is sad that he is leaving.

Nous avons peur qu'il pleuve. (noo zah-von puhr keel pluhv) - We are afraid that it will rain.

In these sentences, the subjunctive is used after expressions of emotion, such as être content(e) que (to be happy that), être triste que (to be sad that), and avoir peur que (to be afraid that).

4. Expressing Necessity or Obligation

The subjunctive is used to express necessity or obligation. Here are some examples:

Il faut que tu finisses ton travail. (eel foh kuh tew fee-neess ton tra-vye) - It is necessary that you finish your work.

Il est important que nous parlions avec elle. (eel eh ahn-por-tahn kuh noo parl-yon ah-vek ell) - It is important that we talk with her.

Il est essentiel qu'ils sachent la vérité. (eel eh eh-sahn-syel keel sash lah vay-ree-tay) - It is essential that they know the truth.

In these sentences, the subjunctive follows expressions of necessity, such as il faut que (it is necessary that), il est important que (it is important that), and il est essentiel que (it is essential that).

5. Expressing Possibility

The subjunctive is also used to express possibilities. Here are some examples:

Il se peut que tu aies raison. (eel suh puh kuh tew ay ray-zon) - It's possible that you are right.

Il est possible qu'elle vienne demain. (eel eh poh-see-bl kel vyen duh-mahn) - It is possible that she will come tomorrow.

Il est improbable qu'il réussisse. (eel eh ehn-pro-bah-bl keel ray-ew-seess) - It is unlikely that he will succeed.

In these sentences, the subjunctive is used after phrases that indicate possibility, like il se peut que (it is possible that), il est possible que (it is possible that), and il est improbable que (it is unlikely that).

Irregular Verbs in the Subjunctive Mood

Just like in other moods, some verbs are irregular in the subjunctive. These verbs don't follow the regular pattern, so you'll need to memorize them. Here are some common irregular verbs in the subjunctive mood:

- **Être** (to be) - que je sois (kuh zhuh swah), que tu sois (kuh tew swah), qu'il/elle soit (keel/ell swah), que nous soyons (kuh noo swah-yon), que vous soyez (kuh voo swah-yay), qu'ils/elles soient (keel/ell swah)

- **Avoir** (to have) - que j'aie (kuh zhay), que tu aies (kuh tew ay), qu'il/elle ait (keel/ell ay), que nous ayons (kuh noo ay-yon), que vous ayez (kuh voo ay-yay), qu'ils/elles aient (keel/ell ay)

- **Faire** (to do/make) - que je fasse (kuh zhuh fass), que tu fasses (kuh tew fass), qu'il/elle fasse (keel/ell fass), que nous fassions (kuh noo fah-syon), que vous fassiez (kuh voo fah-syay), qu'ils/elles fassent (keel/ell fass)

- **Aller** (to go) - que j'aille (kuh zhye), que tu ailles (kuh ty), qu'il/elle aille (keel/ell aye), que nous allions (kuh noo al-yon), que vous alliez (kuh voo al-yay), qu'ils/elles aillent (keel/ell aye)

- **Vouloir** (to want) - que je veuille (kuh zhuh vuh-yuh), que tu veuilles (kuh tew vuh-yuh), qu'il/elle veuille (keel/ell vuh-yuh), que nous voulions (kuh noo voo-lyon), que vous vouliez (kuh voo voo-lyay), qu'ils/elles veuillent (keel/ell vuh-yuh)

These irregular verbs have unique forms in the subjunctive, so it's important to learn them separately.

Using the Subjunctive in Sentences

Let's see how to use the subjunctive in sentences. Here are some examples:

Il faut que je parte maintenant. (eel foh kuh zhuh part mehn-tuh-nahn) - It is necessary that I leave now.

Je souhaite qu'elle réussisse son examen. (zhuh soo-et kel ray-ew-seess sohn eg-zah-mahn) - I wish that she passes her exam.

Il est important que nous soyons honnêtes. (eel eh ahn-por-tahn kuh noo swah-yon oh-net) - It is important that we be honest.

Je doute qu'il dise la vérité. (zhuh doot keel deez lah vay-ree-tay) - I doubt that he is telling the truth.

In these sentences, the subjunctive mood is used to express necessity, wishes, importance, and doubt.

Key Points to Remember:

1. **Formation of Subjunctive Mood:** The subjunctive mood is formed by taking the stem from the "ils/elles" form of the verb in the present tense, removing the "-ent" ending, and adding the subjunctive endings (-e, -es, -e, -ions, -iez, -ent).

2. **When to Use the Subjunctive:** The subjunctive is used in situations involving doubt, wishes, emotions, necessity, and possibilities, typically after certain phrases or verbs that trigger its use.

3. **Expressing Emotions and Wishes:** Use the subjunctive after expressions of emotion or desire, such as "Je veux que" (I want that) or "Je suis content(e) que" (I am happy that).

4. **Irregular Verbs:** Some verbs, like "être," "avoir," "faire," and "aller," have irregular forms in the subjunctive mood and must be memorized.

5. **Polite Requests and Uncertainty:** The subjunctive is also used in polite requests and to express uncertainty or hypothetical situations, making it essential for nuanced communication.

Chapter 41

Prepositions

In this chapter, we're going to learn about **Prepositions** in French. Prepositions are small words that help show the relationship between different parts of a sentence. They often tell us where something is, when something happens, or how things are related to each other. In English, prepositions are words like "in," "on," "at," and "with." Learning prepositions in French will help you describe locations, give directions, and talk about time and relationships. Let's get started!

What Are Prepositions?

A preposition is a word that links a noun, pronoun, or phrase to other parts of a sentence. It helps to show relationships in time, place, direction, and more. For example, in the sentence "The book is on the table," the word "on" is a preposition that shows the relationship between the book and the table.

In French, prepositions work in much the same way, but it's important to learn how they're used and how they might differ from English. Some French prepositions have direct translations in English, while others are used in different ways.

Common French Prepositions

Let's start by learning some of the most common French prepositions and their meanings:

- **À** (ah) - to, at, in
- **De** (duh) - of, from
- **En** (ahn) - in, into
- **Dans** (dahn) - in, inside
- **Sur** (syur) - on, upon
- **Sous** (soo) - under, beneath

- **Avec** (ah-vek) - with

- **Pour** (poor) - for

- **Sans** (sahn) - without

- **Chez** (shay) - at the home of, at (a person's place)

These prepositions are used in everyday conversations to describe locations, relationships, and actions. Let's take a closer look at each one and see how to use them in sentences.

Using "À"

The preposition à is very versatile in French. It can mean "to," "at," or "in" depending on how it's used. Here are some examples:

Je vais à l'école. (zhuh vay ah lay-kohl) - I'm going to school.

Il habite à Paris. (eel ah-beet ah pah-ree) - He lives in Paris.

Nous sommes à la maison. (noo sohm ah lah may-zon) - We are at home.

In these sentences, à is used to indicate direction (going to a place), location (being in a city), and position (being at home).

Using "De"

The preposition de is also very common and is used to show origin, possession, or to describe something. Here are some examples:

Je viens de France. (zhuh vyen duh frahnss) - I come from France.

Le livre de Marie est sur la table. (luh leevr duh mah-ree eh syur lah tah-bluh) - Marie's book is on the table.

C'est un cadeau de mon ami. (say uhn kah-doh duh mohn ah-mee) - It's a gift from my friend.

In these sentences, de is used to indicate origin (coming from a place), possession (belonging to someone), and the source of something (a gift from someone).

Using "En" and "Dans"

Both en and dans can mean "in," but they're used differently. En is used to describe being inside a country, region, or general area, while dans is used for more specific locations. Here are some examples:

Je suis en classe. (zhuh swee ahn klass) - I am in class.

Nous sommes en France. (noo sohm ahn frahnss) - We are in France.

Le livre est dans le sac. (luh leevr eh dahn luh sahk) - The book is in the bag.

Elle est dans la voiture. (ell eh dahn lah vwahr-tyoor) - She is in the car.

Notice how en is used for broader locations (like countries or classrooms), while dans is used for more specific or enclosed spaces (like a bag or a car).

Using "Sur" and "Sous"

The prepositions sur and sous are used to describe things that are on top of or underneath something else. Here are some examples:

Le livre est sur la table. (luh leevr eh syur lah tah-bluh) - The book is on the table.

Le chat est sous la chaise. (luh shah eh soo lah shez) - The cat is under the chair.

In these sentences, sur indicates that something is on top of a surface, and sous indicates that something is underneath or below another object.

Using "Avec" and "Sans"

The prepositions avec and sans are used to describe being with or without something or someone. Here are some examples:

Je vais au cinéma avec mes amis. (zhuh vay oh see-nay-mah ah-vek mayz ah-mee) - I'm going to the movies with my friends.

Elle boit son café sans sucre. (ell bwah sohn kah-fay sahn sookr) - She drinks her coffee without sugar.

In these sentences, avec indicates being together with someone or something, and sans indicates the absence of something.

Using "Pour"

The preposition pour is used to express purpose, intent, or a recipient. Here are some examples:

Ce cadeau est pour toi. (suh kah-doh eh poor twah) - This gift is for you.

Je travaille pour gagner de l'argent. (zhuh tra-vye poor gah-nye duh lar-zhahn) - I work to earn money.

In these sentences, pour is used to indicate the purpose of an action or to show that something is intended for someone.

Using "Chez"

The preposition chez is used to talk about being at someone's house or place of work. Here are some examples:

Je vais chez mon ami. (zhuh vay shay mohn ah-mee) - I'm going to my friend's house.

Elle est chez le médecin. (ell eh shay luh med-sahn) - She is at the doctor's office.

In these sentences, chez is used to indicate that someone is at another person's place or at a professional's office.

Prepositions of Time

Prepositions are also used to talk about time, such as when something happens. Here are some common prepositions of time:

- **À** (ah) - at
- **En** (ahn) - in
- **Depuis** (duh-pwee) - since
- **Pendant** (pahn-dahn) - during
- **Jusqu'à** (zhyoo-skah) - until

Here are some examples of how to use them:

Nous allons partir à cinq heures. (noo zah-lohn par-teer ah sank uhr) - We're going to leave at five o'clock.

Elle est née en 2005. (ell eh nay ahn duh-mil sank) - She was born in 2005.

Je travaille depuis trois heures. (zhuh tra-vye duh-pwee trwa uhr) - I have been working since three o'clock.

Il a dormi pendant le film. (eel ah dor-mee pahn-dahn luh feem) - He slept during the movie.

Ils resteront jusqu'à demain. (eel res-ter-ohn zhyoo-skah duh-mahn) - They will stay until tomorrow.

In these sentences, prepositions like à and en are used to talk about when something happens, while depuis, pendant, and jusqu'à are used to express the duration or timing of events.

Combining Prepositions with Articles

In French, prepositions can combine with definite articles to form contractions. This happens when the preposition à or de comes before the articles le (the) or les (the plural form). Here's how it works:

À + le = au (oh) - to the/at the

À + les = aux (oh) - to the/at the (plural)

De + le = du (dew) - of the/from the

De + les = des (day) - of the/from the (plural)

Here are some examples:

Je vais au parc. (zhuh vay oh park) - I'm going to the park.

Ils parlent aux enfants. (eel parl ohz ahn-fahn) - They are talking to the children.

Il revient du travail. (eel ruh-vyen dew tra-vye) - He's coming back from work.

Nous parlons des livres. (noo parl-on day leevr) - We are talking about the books.

In these sentences, the prepositions à and de combine with the articles le and les to form contractions that make the sentences sound more natural.

Key Points to Remember:

1. **Understanding Prepositions:** Prepositions are small words that connect nouns, pronouns, or phrases to other parts of a sentence, indicating relationships in time, place, direction, and more.

2. **Common French Prepositions:** Key prepositions in French include "à" (to, at, in), "de" (of, from), "en" (in), "dans" (inside), "sur" (on), "sous" (under), "avec" (with), "pour" (for), "sans" (without), and "chez" (at the home of).

3. **Prepositions of Time:** French prepositions like "à" (at), "en" (in), "depuis" (since), "pendant" (during), and "jusqu'à" (until) help describe when events occur or how long they last.

4. **Combining Prepositions with Articles:** Prepositions can combine with definite articles to form contractions, such as "au" (à + le), "aux" (à + les), "du" (de + le), and "des" (de + les).

5. **Usage in Sentences:** Understanding how to use these prepositions helps in describing

locations, giving directions, discussing time, and expressing relationships in French.

Chapter 42

Conjunctions

In this chapter, we're going to learn about **Conjunctions** in French. Conjunctions are words that connect different parts of a sentence. They help you link words, phrases, and clauses together, making your sentences more complex and interesting. In English, conjunctions are words like "and," "but," "or," and "because." Learning conjunctions in French will help you express more complex ideas and join your thoughts smoothly. Let's get started!

What Are Conjunctions?

Conjunctions are words that join different parts of a sentence. They can connect words, phrases, or entire clauses. For example, in the sentence "I like apples and oranges," the word "and" is a conjunction that links the two nouns "apples" and "oranges." In French, conjunctions work similarly, helping you connect ideas and add variety to your sentences.

Common French Conjunctions

Let's start by learning some of the most common French conjunctions and their meanings:

- **Et** (ay) - and

- **Mais** (meh) - but

- **Ou** (oo) - or

- **Parce que** (parss kuh) - because

- **Quand** (kahn) - when

- **Si** (see) - if

- **Ni... ni** (nee... nee) - neither... nor

- **Donc** (dohnk) - so, therefore

- **Puis** (pwee) - then

- **Car** (kar) - because, for

These conjunctions are used every day in French to connect ideas and add depth to your sentences. Let's explore how to use each of them with examples.

Using "Et"

The conjunction et is used to connect words or phrases that are similar or related. It's equivalent to "and" in English. Here are some examples:

J'aime les pommes et les oranges. (zhaym lay pom ay layz oh-rahnzh) - I like apples and oranges.

Elle parle français et anglais. (ell parl frahn-say ay ahn-glay) - She speaks French and English.

Nous avons des chiens et des chats. (noo zah-von day shyan ay day shah) - We have dogs and cats.

In these sentences, et is used to link similar elements, such as nouns, languages, or pets.

Using "Mais"

The conjunction mais is used to introduce a contrast or exception. It's equivalent to "but" in English. Here are some examples:

Je veux sortir, mais il pleut. (zhuh vuh sor-teer, meh eel pluh) - I want to go out, but it's raining.

Il est intelligent, mais paresseux. (eel eh eh-tell-ee-zhahn, meh pah-reh-suh) - He is smart, but lazy.

Nous avons faim, mais il n'y a rien à manger. (noo zah-von fam, meh eel nee ah ryen ah mahn-zhay) - We are hungry, but there is nothing to eat.

In these sentences, mais is used to show a contrast between two ideas or actions.

Using "Ou"

The conjunction ou is used to offer a choice between two or more options. It's equivalent to "or" in English. Here are some examples:

Tu veux du thé ou du café? (tew vuh dew tay oo dew kah-fay) - Do you want tea or coffee?

Nous irons à Paris ou à Lyon cet été. (noo eer-on ah pah-ree oo ah lyee-ohn set ay-tay) - We will go to Paris or Lyon this summer.

Elle préfère lire ou regarder la télévision. (ell pray-fehr leer oo ruh-gar-day lah tay-lay-vee-zyon) - She prefers to read or watch TV.

In these sentences, ou is used to present different options or alternatives.

Using "Parce que"

The conjunction parce que is used to explain the reason for something. It's equivalent to "because" in English. Here are some examples:

Je suis fatigué parce que j'ai mal dormi. (zhuh swee fah-tee-gay parss kuh zhay mal dor-mee) - I'm tired because I slept poorly.

Nous restons à la maison parce qu'il fait froid dehors. (noo res-ton ah lah may-zon parss keel fay frwah duh-or) - We are staying at home because it's cold outside.

Elle est contente parce qu'elle a réussi son examen. (ell eh kohn-tahn parss kel ah ray-ew-see sohn eg-zah-mahn) - She is happy because she passed her exam.

In these sentences, parce que is used to give a reason or cause for an action or situation.

Using "Quand"

The conjunction quand is used to talk about when something happens. It's equivalent to "when" in English. Here are some examples:

Quand il pleut, je reste à la maison. (kahn eel pluh, zhuh rest ah lah may-zon) - When it rains, I stay at home.

Nous partirons quand tu seras prêt. (noo par-teer-on kahn tew suh-rah pray) - We will leave when you are ready.

Elle sourit quand elle entend cette chanson. (ell soo-ree kahn tell ahn-tahn set shan-sohn) - She smiles when she hears this song.

In these sentences, quand is used to indicate the timing of an event or action.

Using "Si"

The conjunction si is used to introduce a condition. It's equivalent to "if" in English. Here are some examples:

Si tu veux, nous pouvons aller au parc. (see tew vuh, noo poo-von zah-lay oh park) - If you want, we can go to the park.

Elle viendra si elle a le temps. (ell vyen-drah see ell ah luh tan) - She will come if she has time.

Je réussirai si je travaille dur. (zhuh ray-ew-see-ray see zhuh tra-vye dur) - I will succeed if I work hard.

In these sentences, si is used to express a condition that needs to be met for something else to happen.

Using "Ni... ni"

The conjunction ni... ni is used to say "neither... nor" in English. It's used to express the absence of both options. Here are some examples:

Je n'aime ni les pommes ni les oranges. (zhuh nem nee lay pom nee layz oh-rahnzh) - I like neither apples nor oranges.

Il ne veut ni sortir ni rester à la maison. (eel nuh vuh nee sor-teer nee res-tay ah lah may-zon) - He wants neither to go out nor to stay at home.

Nous n'avons ni chat ni chien. (noo nah-von nee shah nee shyan) - We have neither a cat nor a dog.

In these sentences, ni... ni is used to negate two options at the same time.

Using "Donc"

The conjunction donc is used to show a logical consequence or conclusion. It's equivalent to "so" or "therefore" in English. Here are some examples:

Il fait froid, donc je mets un manteau. (eel fay frwah, donk zhuh meh uhn mahn-toh) - It's cold, so I'm putting on a coat.

Elle a étudié, donc elle a réussi l'examen. (ell ah eh-too-dyay, donk ell ah ray-ew-see lek-sah-mahn) - She studied, so she passed the exam.

Nous avons faim, donc nous allons manger. (noo zah-von fam, donk noo zah-lon mahn-zhay) - We're hungry, so we're going to eat.

In these sentences, donc is used to connect a cause to its effect or a reason to its outcome.

Using "Puis"

The conjunction puis is used to indicate the next action in a sequence. It's equivalent to "then" in English. Here are some examples:

Je vais à l'école, puis je fais mes devoirs. (zhuh vay ah lay-kohl, pwee zhuh fay may duh-vwahr) - I go to school, then I do my homework.

Elle a pris son petit déjeuner, puis elle est partie. (ell ah pree sohn puh-tee day-zhuh-nay, pwee ell eh par-tee) - She had her breakfast, then she left.

Nous avons joué au parc, puis nous sommes rentrés à la maison. (noo zah-von zhway oh park, pwee noo sohm rahn-tray ah lah may-zon) - We played at the park, then we went home.

In these sentences, puis is used to show the order in which actions occur.

Using "Car"

The conjunction car is similar to parce que and is used to explain the reason for something. It's often translated as "because" or "for" in English. Here are some examples:

Je pars maintenant, car il est tard. (zhuh par mehn-tuh-nahn, kar eel eh tar) - I'm leaving now because it's late.

Nous restons à la maison, car il pleut. (noo res-ton ah lah may-zon, kar eel pluh) - We're staying home because it's raining.

Elle est heureuse, car elle a reçu une bonne nouvelle. (ell eh uh-ruhze, kar ell ah ruh-syoo uhn bon noo-vel) - She is happy because she received good news.

In these sentences, car is used to provide an explanation or reason for something.

Key Points to Remember:

1. **Understanding Conjunctions:** Conjunctions are words that connect different parts of a sentence, such as words, phrases, or clauses, making sentences more complex and cohesive.

2. **Common French Conjunctions:** Important French conjunctions include "et" (and), "mais" (but), "ou" (or), "parce que" (because), and "si" (if), which help link ideas and express conditions, reasons, and choices.

3. **Using "Et" and "Mais":** "Et" is used to connect similar elements, while "mais" introduces contrast or exceptions in a sentence.

4. **Using "Parce que" and "Si":** "Parce que" explains reasons, and "si" introduces conditions, both of which are essential for expressing cause and effect or hypothetical situations.

5. **Adding Depth to Sentences:** Conjunctions like "donc" (so) and "puis" (then) help to show logical consequences and sequence of actions, enriching your ability to convey more complex thoughts.

Chapter 43

Indirect and Direct Object Pronouns

In this chapter, we're going to learn about **Indirect and Direct Object Pronouns** in French. These pronouns are used to replace nouns in a sentence to avoid repetition and make your sentences smoother. Understanding how to use these pronouns will help you speak and write French more naturally. Let's dive in!

What Are Direct and Indirect Object Pronouns?

First, let's clarify what direct and indirect objects are. A **direct object** is the person or thing that directly receives the action of the verb. For example, in the sentence "I see the dog," the dog is the direct object because it receives the action of seeing.

An **indirect object** is the person or thing that receives the direct object. For example, in the sentence "I give the book to my friend," the book is the direct object (what is being given), and "my friend" is the indirect object (who is receiving the book).

In French, instead of repeating the noun, we use pronouns to replace these objects. This makes sentences shorter and less repetitive.

Direct Object Pronouns in French

Here are the direct object pronouns in French:

- **Me** (muh) - me
- **Te** (tuh) - you (informal)
- **Le** (luh) - him, it (masculine)
- **La** (lah) - her, it (feminine)
- **Nous** (noo) - us

- **Vous** (voo) - you (formal or plural)
- **Les** (lay) - them

Let's see how these pronouns are used in sentences:

Je vois le chien. (zhuh vwah luh shyen) - I see the dog.

Je le vois. (zhuh luh vwah) - I see it.

Here, the noun le chien (the dog) is replaced by the direct object pronoun le (it), because the dog is the direct object of the verb voir (to see).

Another example:

Elle aime la chanson. (ell em lah shahn-sohn) - She loves the song.

Elle l'aime. (ell lem) - She loves it.

In this case, the noun la chanson (the song) is replaced by the direct object pronoun la (it).

Indirect Object Pronouns in French

Here are the indirect object pronouns in French:

- **Me** (muh) - to me
- **Te** (tuh) - to you (informal)
- **Lui** (lwee) - to him, to her
- **Nous** (noo) - to us
- **Vous** (voo) - to you (formal or plural)
- **Leur** (luhr) - to them

Let's see how these pronouns are used in sentences:

Je donne le livre à Marie. (zhuh don luh leevr ah mah-ree) - I give the book to Marie.

Je lui donne le livre. (zhuh lwee don luh leevr) - I give her the book.

In this example, the indirect object à Marie (to Marie) is replaced by the indirect object pronoun lui (to her).

Another example:

Nous parlons à nos amis. (noo par-lon ah noh zah-mee) - We talk to our friends.

Nous leur parlons. (noo luhr par-lon) - We talk to them.

Here, the indirect object à nos amis (to our friends) is replaced by the indirect object pronoun leur (to them).

Position of Direct and Indirect Object Pronouns

In French, both direct and indirect object pronouns are placed before the verb. This is different from English, where object pronouns typically come after the verb. Let's look at some examples:

Je vois le chien. (zhuh vwah luh shyen) - I see the dog.

Je le vois. (zhuh luh vwah) - I see it.

Notice that le comes before the verb voir (to see).

Another example:

Elle donne les fleurs à sa mère. (ell don lay flur ah sah mehr) - She gives the flowers to her mother.

Elle lui donne les fleurs. (ell lwee don lay flur) - She gives her the flowers.

Here, lui (to her) is placed before the verb donner (to give).

Using Both Direct and Indirect Object Pronouns Together

Sometimes, you need to use both direct and indirect object pronouns in the same sentence. In French, the order of the pronouns is important. The indirect object pronoun comes before the direct object pronoun. Let's see how this works:

Il donne le livre à Marie. (eel don luh leevr ah mah-ree) - He gives the book to Marie.

Il le lui donne. (eel luh lwee don) - He gives it to her.

In this example, le (it) is the direct object pronoun, and lui (to her) is the indirect object pronoun. Notice how lui comes before le.

Another example:

Je prête les clés à mon frère. (zhuh pret lay klay ah mohn frehr) - I lend the keys to my brother.

Je les lui prête. (zhuh lay lwee pret) - I lend them to him.

Here, les (them) is the direct object pronoun, and lui (to him) is the indirect object pronoun. Again, lui comes before les.

Agreement with Direct Object Pronouns

In the passé composé (a common past tense in French), the past participle must agree in gender and number with the direct object pronoun if it comes before the verb. Let's see how this works:

J'ai vu les filles. (zhay voo lay fee) - I saw the girls.

Je les ai vues. (zhuh lay zay vyoo) - I saw them.

In this example, les (them) refers to les filles (the girls), which is feminine plural. The past participle vu (seen) becomes vues to agree with the feminine plural direct object pronoun les.

Another example:

Elle a acheté la robe. (ell ah ah-shay-tay lah rob) - She bought the dress.

Elle l'a achetée. (ell lah ah-shay-tay) - She bought it.

Here, la (it) refers to la robe (the dress), which is feminine singular. The past participle acheté (bought) becomes achetée to agree with the feminine singular direct object pronoun la.

Key Points to Remember:

1. **Direct Object Pronouns:** These pronouns replace nouns directly receiving the action of the verb (e.g., "le," "la," "les"). They are placed before the verb in French sentences.

2. **Indirect Object Pronouns:** These pronouns replace nouns that receive the direct object (e.g., "lui," "leur"). Like direct object pronouns, they also come before the verb.

3. **Position of Pronouns:** Both direct and indirect object pronouns are positioned before the verb in French, unlike in English.

4. **Using Both Pronouns Together:** When using both direct and indirect object pronouns in a sentence, the indirect pronoun comes before the direct pronoun (e.g., "Je le lui donne").

5. **Agreement in Passé Composé:** In the passé composé, the past participle agrees in gender and number with the direct object pronoun if it precedes the verb (e.g., "Je les ai vues").

Chapter 44

Advanced Grammar Rules

In this chapter, we're going to explore some **Advanced Grammar Rules** in French. These rules will help you refine your language skills and understand more complex structures in French. Don't worry if they seem challenging at first; with practice, you'll get the hang of them. Let's dive in!

1. Agreement of Past Participles with "Être"

In the passé composé, when you use the verb être (to be) as the auxiliary verb, the past participle must agree in gender and number with the subject of the sentence. This is different from using avoir (to have) as the auxiliary verb, where no agreement is needed unless there's a direct object pronoun before the verb.

For example:

Elle est allée à l'école. (ell eh ah-lay ah lay-kohl) - She went to school.

Ils sont partis hier. (eel sohn par-tee yair) - They left yesterday.

In these sentences, the past participles allée (gone) and partis (left) agree with the subjects elle (she) and ils (they). Allée is feminine singular, matching elle, and partis is masculine plural, matching ils.

2. Subjunctive Mood

The subjunctive mood is used to express doubts, wishes, emotions, and uncertainty. It's often introduced by phrases like il faut que (it is necessary that), je veux que (I want that), or bien que (although).

For example:

Il faut que tu viennes. (eel foh kuh tew vyen) - You need to come.

Je veux que tu sois heureux. (zhuh vuh kuh tew swahz uh-ruh) - I want you to be happy.

In these sentences, the verbs viennes (come) and sois (be) are in the subjunctive mood because they follow expressions of necessity and desire.

3. Use of "Y" and "En"

French has two special pronouns, y and en, which are used to replace phrases involving location, quantity, or other expressions. Understanding when and how to use these pronouns can make your sentences smoother and more concise.

Y

The pronoun y replaces phrases that begin with à (to) or other prepositions indicating a place, such as dans (in), chez (at someone's place), and sur (on). It means "there" in English.

For example:

Je vais à Paris. (zhuh vay ah pah-ree) - I am going to Paris.

J'y vais. (zhee vay) - I'm going there.

Here, y replaces à Paris (to Paris).

En

The pronoun en replaces phrases that begin with de (of, from) and those that involve quantities. It can mean "some," "of it," or "of them" in English.

For example:

Tu veux du pain? (tew vuh dew pan) - Do you want some bread?

J'en veux. (zhahn vuh) - I want some.

Here, en replaces du pain (some bread).

4. Inversion in Questions

In formal French, especially in writing, questions can be formed by inverting the subject and the verb. This is more common in formal situations or written French.

For example:

Tu vas au cinéma? (tew vah oh see-nay-mah) - Are you going to the movies?

Vas-tu au cinéma? (vah tew oh see-nay-mah) - Are you going to the movies?

In the second sentence, the subject tu and the verb vas are inverted to form a more formal question.

5. Relative Pronouns: Qui, Que, Dont, Où

Relative pronouns are used to link two clauses together, giving more information about a noun mentioned in the first clause. The most common relative pronouns are qui, que, dont, and où.

Qui

Qui is used as a subject and can mean "who" or "which."

For example:

La fille qui parle est ma sœur. (lah fee kee parl eh mah suhr) - The girl who is speaking is my sister.

Que

Que is used as a direct object and can mean "whom" or "that."

For example:

Le livre que j'ai lu est intéressant. (luh leevr kuh zhay loo eh eh-teh-reh-sahn) - The book that I read is interesting.

Dont

Dont is used to indicate possession or relationship, and it can mean "whose," "of which," or "about which."

For example:

La femme dont je parle est médecin. (lah fam dohn zhuh parl eh med-sahn) - The woman I'm talking about is a doctor.

Où

Où is used to indicate a place or time, and it can mean "where" or "when."

For example:

La maison où j'habite est grande. (lah may-zon oo zhah-beet eh grahnd) - The house where I live is big.

6. Passive Voice

The passive voice is used when the focus is on the action rather than who is performing it. In French, the passive voice is formed using the verb être followed by the past participle of the main verb.

For example:

Le gâteau est fait par Marie. (luh gah-toh eh feh par mah-ree) - The cake is made by Marie.

In this sentence, the focus is on the cake (the action) rather than Marie (the doer).

7. The Conditional Perfect

The conditional perfect is used to express what would have happened under different circumstances. It's formed by using the conditional form of avoir or être followed by the past participle of the main verb.

For example:

J'aurais fini mes devoirs, mais j'étais trop fatigué. (zhaw-ray fee-nee may duh-vwahr, meh zhay-tay troh fah-tee-gay) - I would have finished my homework, but I was too tired.

In this sentence, the conditional perfect j'aurais fini expresses an action that could have happened but didn't because of a specific reason.

8. Si Clauses

Si clauses are used to express conditions. There are three main types of si clauses:

Si + Present Tense + Future Tense

This is used for real conditions that are likely to happen.

For example:

Si tu étudies, tu réussiras. (see tew eh-tew-dee, tew ray-ew-see-rah) - If you study, you will succeed.

Si + Imperfect Tense + Conditional Tense

This is used for hypothetical conditions that are possible but not certain.

For example:

Si j'avais de l'argent, je voyagerais. (see zhah-vay duh lar-zhahn, zhuh vwa-yah-zhuh-ray) - If I had money, I would travel.

Si + Pluperfect Tense + Past Conditional Tense

This is used for hypothetical conditions that are impossible or did not happen.

For example:

Si j'avais su, je ne serais pas venu. (see zhah-vay soo, zhuh nuh suh-ray pah vuh-nyoo) - If I had known, I wouldn't have come.

Key Points to Remember:

1. **Agreement of Past Participles with "Être":** In the passé composé, when using "être" as the auxiliary verb, the past participle must agree in gender and number with the subject of the sentence.

2. **Subjunctive Mood:** The subjunctive mood is used to express doubts, wishes, emotions, and uncertainty. It often follows phrases like "il faut que" or "je veux que."

3. **Use of "Y" and "En":** The pronouns "y" and "en" replace phrases related to location, quantity, or other expressions, helping to make sentences more concise.

4. **Inversion in Questions:** In formal French, questions can be formed by inverting the subject and verb, especially in writing or formal speech.

5. **Relative Pronouns (Qui, Que, Dont, Où):** These pronouns are used to link clauses and provide more information about a noun, with each serving a different purpose (e.g., "qui" for subjects, "que" for direct objects).